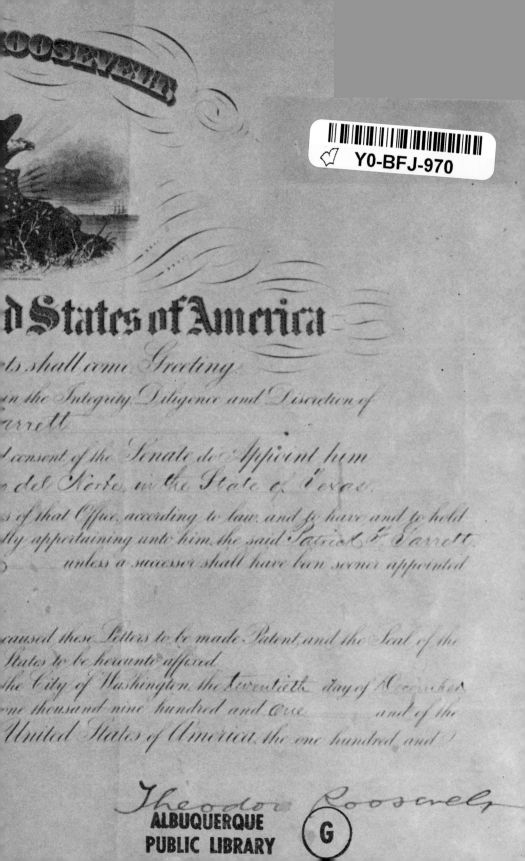

GARRETT
and
ROOSEVELT

by

Jack DeMattos

THE
EARLY WEST

CREATIVE PUBLISHING COMPANY
BOX 9292, PHONE 409-775-6047
COLLEGE STATION, TEXAS 77840

DeMattos, Jack, 1944-
    Garrett and Roosevelt / Jack DeMattos.
    181 p.
    Bibliography: p. 167
    Includes index
    ISBN 0-932702-42-2
    1. Garrett, Pat F. (Pat Floyd), 1850-1908—Career
in Customs Service. 2. Roosevelt, Theodore, 1858-1919—
Friends and associates. 3. U.S. Customs Service—Officials
and employees—Selection and appointment. I. Title.
F801.G3D46 1988
973.91'1'0922--dc 19   87-36530, CIP

Copyrighted by Creative Publishing Company, 1988.
Box 9292, Ph. 409-775-6047, College Station, Texas
77840

This book is published as a limited edition
of seven hundred and fifty numbered copies.

This is Number **427** of 750

Dedicated to
my wife,
Sandi

TABLE OF CONTENTS

INTRODUCTION
by
Leon C. Metz

Pat Garrett and Theodore Roosevelt changed our world. Garrett did so as the stove-pipe thin sheriff who fired a bullet through the heart of Billy the Kid in 1881. That gunshot created what historian Robert M. Utley called, "one of the mightiest legends of all time."

Roosevelt was famous for his personal philosophy of "speak softly but carry a big stick." He represented the last reach of American imperialism, an adventurous scholar who considered pluck and courage the epitome of American virtue.

Although they obviously knew each other by reputation for many years, the Garrett-Roosevelt relationship took-off in late 1901. Garrett was on a downhill slide and desperately needing a job. Roosevelt was trying to act responsibly as President, yet appointing to office men whose backgrounds teemed with turmoil, discord and violence.

Still, Garrett was more than just a manslayer. He had been a loyal party man, serving in various layers of territorial government. He spoke well on his feet and could debate ideas as well as philosophies. His Spanish was fluent, he had met presidents and governors, and was on a first-name basis with every political and civic leader in the southwest and throughout much of the nation. His integrity and honesty probably matched Roosevelt's, although each had different limitations, standards and strains.

Garrett was also a visionary and tempermental gambler with a biting sense of humor. Enemies outnumbered friends. He didn't compromise easily. Two of his great strengths were loyalty and family. One of his major weaknesses was failing to cut himself loose from odious relationships, specifically the one with Tom Powers, a saloon owner whose friendship eventually led to Pat's failure to be reappointed as Collector of Customs in El Paso, Texas.

Jack DeMattos has perfectly captured the stormy and controversial years of Pat Garrett's tenure as customs collector from 1902 into January 1906. We see Pat Garrett beset by powerful and influential political enemies, a public servant unsophisticated enough to be anything other than his own worst adversary.

We watch a Roosevelt agonizing over decisions, sensing even in the beginning that the appointment of Garrett is a mistake. The President repeatedly ignored the logic of his own intellect and found reliance in his often faulty admiration of active, and occasionally primitive, men.

Yet, it is rare to find two people, so distant in social, cultural and educational refinements, to have been so trapped in similar worlds. Pat Garrett and Theodore Roosevelt could have switched lives given a different set of circumstances.

Furthermore, there are elements of Greek tragedy in the Pat Garrett—Theodore Roosevelt history. It is present not only in the evaluations of DeMattos, but in the telegrams, letters, government reports, newspaper articles, interviews. Such complete and diverse documentation rarely exists on any subject of the American West.

DeMattos tells a good story, one carefully constructed and well organized. What emerges, however, is more than an essay about two significant and aggressive individuals. Their struggle for an accommodation with each other, and with themselves, is a microcosm of early 20th century politics that could just as easily have been played out in New York City or Washington, D. C.

Garrett and Roosevelt is a unique and intriguing tale. I wish I had written it.

Leon C. Metz
El Paso, Texas
January, 1988

ACKNOWLEDGEMENTS

My most obvious debt is to Theodore Roosevelt, whose unusual friendship with several gunmen inspired this second volume of the "White House Gunfighters" trilogy. Next in order are my publishers, Jim and Theresa Earle, who have made it possible to share the story of *Garrett and Roosevelt* with you.

Invaluable assistance was provided by Wallace Finley Dailey, curator of the Theodore Roosevelt Collection at Harvard, as well as Phyllis E. McLaughlin of the Iowa State Historical Department and Margaret Foster of Des Moines, Iowa.

Historian Joseph G. Rosa of England has been a constant source of information, inspiration and encouragement during this and numerous other projects. A note of thanks is also due to Ed Doherty, my friend and editor at *Real West*, as well as to historians Glenn G. Boyer, Robert K. DeArment, Leon C. Metz, Robert F. Palmquist, William B. Secrest, Joseph W. Snell and Al Turner.

For their friendship, suggestions and encouragement I would also like to thank Don and Fran Barnes, the late Don Bridges, Tim Conroy, Jim and Joanne Dion, Cliff Erickson, Rick Foster, Helen Garant, Bill and Ruby Kelly, Tom and Mary Ann Libby, Irving Metzman, Dave and June O'Leary, Charlie and Donna Scott, Marty and Sandy Singley and Dick Weatherford.

This list would not be complete without mentioning my immediate family—my wife, Sandi, and our children, Dawn and Greg—who have endured my "hobby" of western history and shared me with a typewriter longer than either they or I care to remember.

Thank you—one and all,

Jack DeMattos

Patrick Floyd Jarvis Garrett (1850-1908)

Chapter 1

CONSIDERATION FOR OFFICE

On July 14, 1881, a young man named Henry McCarty entered a bedroom and was shot dead by Sheriff Pat Garrett of Lincoln County, New ,Mexico Territory. As far as western history is concerned, it was a shot that is still being heard around the world.

The killing of Henry McCarty (alias William H.· Bonney, alias Billy the Kid) brought his slayer much in the way of fame, but little in the way of fortune. During the twenty years that followed the Kid's death, Pat Garrett became involved in several unsuccessful commercial enterprises, resulting in sporadic employment.

Because of his large and ever-growing family (he and his wife, Apolinaria, had eight children between 1881 and 1905), Pat Garrett was always short of cash.

By 1901, Pat Garrett cast his eye upon a federal appointment. Garrett knew of President Theodore Roosevelt's love of westerners and figured that his notoriety from killing the Kid gave him a better-than-even chance of getting on the government payroll. Unlike the other "White House Gunfighters," Garrett had not known Roosevelt from the days "when"—but he did have one ace in the hole—influential friends.

One of the most influential—and powerful—of the friends was Albert Bacon Fall.[1] The two had been on opposite sides in the recent past, and Fall seemed an unlikely booster for Garrett's fortunes. Nonetheless, he quickly went to work getting endorsements for Garrett such as the one from an Arizona pal:

Frank Cox
Attorney at Law
307-309 Fleming Block,
Phoenix, Arizona.

December 5, 1901

TO THE PRESIDENT,
Washington, D. C.

Sir:

I take pleasure in recommending to you, as a man of nerve, ability and unquestioned integrity, as far as my information or acquaintance with him goes, Mr. Patrick F. Garrett of Las Cruces, N.M.

I do not know if Mr. Garrett is a candidate for any appointment at your hands, but have been requested by one of his friends to forward a letter in his behalf.

I feel confident, should Mr. Garrett make application for any appointment, that he will be thoroughly capable and will discharge the duties of the office fearlessly and to the best interest of the Government, reflecting credit upon himself and the authority that puts him in office.

I have the honor to be,

Most obediently,

FRANK COX

President Bar Ass'n
of Arizona

The position Garrett had his eye on was that of Collector of Customs for El Paso—a position that had been occupied for three years by a McKinley appointee named H. M. Dillon. A delegation of pro-Garrett lobbyists sought—and received—appointments with President Roosevelt to endorse Garrett for the post; among them was former New Mexico Governor Lew Wallace.[2] Also among the President's visitors during that hectic week was a very concerned H. M. Dillon, the incumbent Collector of Customs for El Paso.

Suddenly, the rumor of Pat Garrett's possible appointment was leaked to the press; although there is no way of knowing just who the Edwardian "Deep Throat" may have been— Albert Bacon Fall seems the most likely candidate. The first report of the developments was contained on page one of the December 12, 1901, issue of the El Paso *Herald*:

PAT GARRETT

Believed To Have Been Decided Upon For The Post Of

COLLECTOR OF CUSTOMS AT EL PASO.

His Interests Looked After By Solomon Luna
and Sheriff Hubbell.

Supported By Gen. Lew Wallace.

It is Said That The Nomination Will Be Sent
To The Senate In A Day Or Two.

Special To The Herald.

WASHINGTON, D.C., December 12—It is stated on reliable authority that President Roosevelt decided today to appoint Patrick F. Garrett of Las Cruces, New Mexico, to be collector of customs at the port of El Paso, for the districts of New Mexico and western Texas.

The nomination, it is announced, will be sent to the senate in a day or two.

Garrett hails from Bernalillo county, New Mexico. He has been here for several days, and has brought to bear upon the president the strongest personal influence, also political, from the territory.

The ex-sheriff's interests have been in charge of Solomon Luna and Sheriff Thomas S. Hubbell of Albuquerque, and among those who have seen and talked with the president in his behalf is Gen. Lew Wallace, who was governor of New Mexico for a long time, and had occasion to see and know something of Pat. Garrett and his work during the fierce border wars incident to the bloody career of Billy the Kid.

Garrett is known all over the country as the "man that killed Billy the Kid," and General Wallace doubtless made the most of Garrett's career as a fearless officer of the law, in presenting his case to the President.

Messrs. Hubbell and Luna were with the President quite awhile yesterday, and they strongly urged the President to name Garrett at once. The President preferred to wait a day or two, but there seems to be no doubt about the appointment being made. The President, it is said, was highly pleased with Garrett's qualifications.

It is certain at least that Garrett is very strong for the office. Whether there is time for any change of plan can only be surmised, and it is well understood here now that Bruce of Texas, who was formerly mentioned as in the lead, will stand no chance.

Among the President's callers yesterday was former Collector of Customs Dillon, of El Paso. He refused to say what he went for or what he got.

The report that the President has decided to appoint Pat Garrett to the position of collector of this port is causing a great deal of comment among those who have taken an interest in the matter. A number of citizens were seen this afternoon and had the following to say:

Judge Harper: "He made a good sheriff in New Mexico. What kind of a collector he would make I do not know."

N. Lapowski: "I am still a candidate for the office. I do not think Garrett has been appointed. I have it on good authority that he is after the office of United States Marshal of New Mexico."

Postmaster Campbell: "He is a good man for the place. He is a candidate and I think he has been appointed."

Deputy United States Marshal Hillebrand: "Pat Garrett suits me."

Acting Collector Townsend: "He is a man of pleasing address and would make a good collector."

Inspector Mehan: "New Mexico has good title to the position. The district includes all of the territory."

Inspector Malloy: "It would not surprise me if more definite information confirming this report of the appointment received."

The lack of certainty caused many to refuse to express their opinion at this time.

Governor Lew Wallace, author of BEN HUR, endorsed Pat Garrett's appointment as customs collector.

NOTES

1. Albert Bacon Fall, the son of a Confederate officer, was born in Frankfort, Kentucky, on November 26, 1861. A sickly youth, he went west for his health and found employment as a cowpuncher and sheepherder in Texas and the Indian Territory. While working as a chuck-wagon cook, he met the local schoolmarm, Emma Garland Morgan, whom he married on May 7, 1883. Soon after their marriage, the newlyweds settled in the silver mining camp of Kingston, New Mexico.

In Kingston, Fall worked as a "mucker" in the famous Bridal Chamber Mine. While thus employed he formed a close friendship with a young miner named Edward L. Doheny (1856-1935). At that time there was little to indicate the great personal power that Fall and Doheny would both one day achieve or that they would go on to become the leading lights of a Presidential scandal.

In 1889 Albert B. Fall hung out his lawyer's shingle in Las Cruces, New Mexico. The town was solidly Republican, firmly under the control of Colonel Albert Jennings Fountain. Since Fall was still a Democrat, he and Colonel Fountain became natural enemies. Among the first to come to Fall's aid in his political battles with Fountain was a wealthy gunfighter named Oliver M. Lee.

When Lee threw his support behind Fall in the 1892 election, Fountain's Republicans became so alarmed that they called on the militia to guard the polls. Fall countered by positioning Lee and several gunmen on various Las Cruces rooftops.

The militia arrived under the command of William H. H. Llewellyn, and Fall stepped into the road and yelled, "Llewellyn, get the hell out of here with that damned militia or I will have you killed!"

The militia reluctantly departed and the Republicans lost the election.

President Grover Clevelend appointed Fall an Associate Justice of New Mexico's Third Judicial District in 1893. He resigned after two years to return to private practice.

After John Selman killed the notorious John Wesley Hardin on August 19, 1895, he employed Fall as his lawyer. Selman's trial resulted in a hung jury and Selman was himself murdered before the case could be rescheduled.

On September 5, 1895, Fall had his lone "gunfight" when he wounded Ben Williams (later a deputy under Pat Garrett) in the arm. Although the incident was clearly an assassination attempt by Fall, the grand jury not only turned him loose, but returned a true bill against Williams and named Albert Jennings Fountain as an accessory!

On January 31, 1896, Colonel Albert Jennings Fountain and his eight-year-old son Henry disappeared on the edge of the White Sands in southern New Mexico. The Fountain mystery failed to be resolved by either the Pinkertons or Apache Indian scouts, when Pat Garrett was sent for. During April, 1896, Garrett was appointed Sheriff of Dona Ana County to fill an unexpired term. It would take Sheriff Garrett two long years before he gathered sufficient evidence in the Fountain case to make arrests.

Finally, on April 2, 1898, Garrett went before Judge Frank W. Parker in Las Cruces, New Mexico, asking for bench warrants to arrest Oliver M. Lee, William McNew, Bill Carr and James Gililland. Within hours, Garrett arrested McNew and Carr. Capturing Lee and Gililland would not be as simple. During the early morning hours of July 12, 1898, Garrett and his posse confronted Lee and Gililland at a spot called Wildy Well near Orogrande, Texas.

During a shootout between the posse and the fugitives, one of Garrett's deputies was mortally wounded. Because of his concern for his dying deputy, Garrett arranged a truce and withdrew from the scene. After the debacle, Garrett endured harsh criticism for not having stood his ground and capturing the fugitives. Both Lee and Gililland remained at large for another eight months, when they finally surrendered to Sheriff George Curry, who had been a Rough Rider with Teddy Roosevelt.

The trial of Lee and Gililland opened on May 25, 1899. The defense attorney was none other than Albert Bacon Fall, who cross-examined both Pat Garrett and George Curry. Eighteen days after the trial began, the case went to the jury, and the defendants were found not guilty. To this day, the murder of Colonel Albert Jennings Fountain remains—officially—unsolved.

With his enemy Fountain out of the way, Fall realized that the time was ripe to improve his political fortunes by joining the ranks of the Republicans—which he did in 1900. He rose like a rocket within the Republican organization. Within a year Fall was important enough to be able to introduce Pat Garrett to President Roosevelt, as well as engineer Garrett's appointment as Collector of Customs in El Paso.

Despite his prominence, a sinister shadow clung to Fall throughout his long life. Among other things, he was suspected of having engineered the December 29, 1908, assassination of Emmanuel "Mannie" Clements Jr.—because of the long-standing grudge Clements held over Fall for defending the killer of his "Uncle Wes" Hardin.

Fall continued his political career as Governor George Curry's Attorney General for New Mexico. Curry was Roosevelt's hand-picked choice for Governor, but Curry's choice of Fall for Attorney General failed to "dee-light" the toothy President. Fall also played a part in the final chapter of Pat Garrett's life by serving as Wayne Brazel's defense attorney and getting his client sprung.

When New Mexico became a state in 1912, Fall became one of its United States Senators and was re-elected in 1918. With the 1920 election of Warren G. Harding to the Presidency, Fall became Secretary of the Interior. The inept Harding wanted to make Fall Secretary of State—but cooler heads prevailed.

As Secretary of the Interior, Fall handed out government oil leases to his old friend Edward L. Doheny and to a prominent oilman named Harry Sinclair, who received the lease to the reserve at Teapot Dome, Wyoming. A national scandal erupted, with Fall being accused of receiving a $100,000 bribe which he termed a "loan." Fall had poured his "loan" into a cattle empire he was planning around the area of Three Rivers, New Mexico.

In 1929 Fall was found guilty of accepting a bribe. When he appealed his case in 1931, the conviction against him was upheld. Fall was sentenced to serve a year and a day at the New Mexico State Penitentiary in Santa Fe. He was the first cabinet officer in the history of the United States to be imprisoned and held that dubious distinction until something called Watergate happened.

After his release, Albert Bacon Fall lived in disgrace for another dozen years. As a final blow, a Doheny-controlled company seized his beloved ranch. Fall died just four days after his eighty-third birthday on November 30, 1944.

2. Lew Wallace was born in Brockville, Indiana, on April 10, 1827. During the Civil War he served with the Union army, and was discharged with the rank of Major General. After Lincoln's assassination, Wallace was one of nine officers who served at the military trial of the individuals accused of conspiring with John Wilkes Booth to murder the President.

Wallace voted for the death penalty, and the execution of George Atzerodt, Lewis Paine, Mary E. Surratt and David E. Herold was carried out on July 7, 1865. Wallace subsequently served as President of the commission which tried Captain Henry Wirz, of Andersonville fame. Wirz was found guilty and executed on November 10, 1865.

Between 1866 and 1867 Wallace was active in Mexican politics, supporting the forces of Benito Juarez against those of the Archduke Maximilian. After Maximilian's execution, Wallace returned to Indiana where he practiced law and made an unsuccessful run for Congress in 1870.

Wallace's first novel, *The Fair God*, was published in 1873 but met with little success. Following the election of Rutherford B. Hayes to the Presidency, Wallace mounted a campaign for a federal appointment. He was hoping for an ambassadorship in Europe or South America but got the Governor's chair in New Mexico instead.

Lew Wallace was sworn in as Governor of New Mexico on September 30, 1878, and served until March 17, 1881. It was during that period that Wallace had his famous face-to-face meeting with Billy the Kid, which has been written about countless times—enough, at least, that it should require no repetition here. It was also during this period that Wallace became aware of the young six-foot-five Sheriff of Lincoln County who would eventually end the Kid's career once and for all—Pat Garrett.

Despite being at the scene of some of the most colorful events in western history, the fact remains that Governor Wallace was far more concerned with the manuscript of his latest novel than he was with the fortunes of either Pat Garrett or Billy the Kid. The novel, *Ben-Hur*, turned out to be one of the most successful ever and has been in nearly continuous print since it was first published by Harper & Brothers on November 12, 1880.

A few months after he resigned as Governor of New Mexico, Wallace was appointed Minister to Turkey and served in that capacity until 1885. During his final years, Wallace produced another novel, *The Prince of India*, and worked on an autobiography that was published a year after he died in 1905.

Lieutenant Colonel Theodore Roosevelt as a member of the "Rough Riders." This photograph was taken in 1898 when Roosevelt was second in command under Colonel Leonard Wood.

Chapter 2

RECOMMENDED FOR OFFICE

If Pat Garrett was blessed with powerful friends, he was likewise cursed with equally powerful enemies. When the first news of the impending appointment leaked out, the Garrett haters lost no time in firing off a salvo of indignant missives to the White House. From the many telegrams of protest that were received, we offer the following as a representative sampling:

Dallas, Texas
Dec. 12, 1901

The President:

My information is that the appointment of Pat. Garrett for collector of customs at El Paso would reflect no credit on your administration, and desire that the matter be held up until I can write you.

GEORGE A. KNIGHT

Late Delegate to
Philada. Convention.

El Paso, Texas
Dec. 12, 1901

The President:

All republicans and majority business men and citizens both parties urge appointment of a Texas collector customs here.

C. W. MURRAY

Secretary
Republican Committee.

El Paso, Texas
December 12, 1901

President Roosevelt:

By all means appoint a Texas man collector of customs here.

M. B. HAWKINS
J. H. MASON

Waco, Texas
December 12, 1901.

Theodore Roosevelt, White House:

Respectfully request Mr. Garrett be not appointed collector at El Paso.

CHAS. A. BOYNTON

Member,
State Executive Committee,
11th Dist.

Houston, Texas
December 12, 1901

President Roosevelt:

Am sure investigation will convince you that Garrett would be unfit for Collector El Paso; few days delay will develop fact.

S. B. STRANG

Brenham, Texas
Dec. 12, 1901

His Excellency,
President Theodore Roosevelt,
Washington, D. C.

In the name of the Republican party of Texas allow me to protest the appointment of any one outside of a Texan for the Collectorship of El Paso.

Patrick Floyd Garrett,
probably taken in
Uvalde, Texas,
in about 1895.

Garrett not suited and we ask you *under no circumstances to make the appointment* of any one but a Texas man. A Republican first, last and all the time, from our State. We have plenty.

More protests to follow.

WM. E. DWYER

Chmn. Nineteenth
Senate Dist.

Rusk, Texas
Dec. 12, 1901

The President:

The appointment of *Garrett, non-resident* as collector at El Paso is *repugnant* to Texas republicans. Texas has material of merit and ability who are entitled to recognition.

THEO. MILLER

Republican State
Executive Committee.

Alpine, Texas
Dec. 12, 1901

Hon. Theodore Roosevelt:

As chairman Brewster County Republican Committee I *protest against* appointment of Mr. Garrett of New Mexico as collector at El Paso, Tex.

D. B. HOARNBECK

Ennis, Texas
December 12, 1901

The President:

Garrett totally unfit for collectorship. I protest against his appointment. Beg you to appoint Texas man.

A. M. MORRISON

Member State Rep.
Committee

Jacksonville, Fla.,
Dec. 12, 1901

The President:

I respectfully but urgently protest against appointment of Mr.

Garrett of New Mexico as collector El Paso, account unfitness. Details
follow later. Nothing but interest of party in South actuates me.

Cecil A. Lyon

Chairman Republican
State Executive Committee,
Texas.

Temple, Tex.
December 12, 1901.

Sec'y Treas'y,
Washington, D. C.

Many loyal citizens of Texas regardless of party will regret
necessity for appointment outsider Garrett Collector El Paso believing
that home rule is best policy when abundance of competent men can
be found at home. Garrett wholly unknown to people and republicans
of State and in my opinion not qualified politically or otherwise for
office.

T. J. DARLIN

County Chairman.

Before the White House telegrapher had a chance to catch
his breath, another batch of protest messages burned up the
wires the following day. Here are a few that were typical:

Henderson, Texas
Dec. 13, 1901.

The President:

Garrett is totally unfit for collector of El Paso. His appointment
would have a bad effect on the party here. Texas is full of good men
and feels that she is entitled to the place.

C. C. FLANAGAN

Member Republican
State Ex. Com.

Hamilton, Texas
Dec. 13, 1901.

President Roosevelt:

Texas people endorse your action generally but want Texas man for collector at El Paso. Garrett of New Mexico not qualified and his appointment would be an injustice to Texas.

JOE E. WILLIAMS

Member State Ex. Committee.

El Paso, Texas
December 13, 1901.

Theodore Roosevelt:

Have labored here thirteen years in interest republicanism and clean politics, expended money and time liberally in making representative newspaper. Delay appointment Garrett, for collector, until El Paso is heard.

J. A. SMITH	ADOLPH KRAUKER
W. S. McCUTHION	HENRY L. CAPELL
HORACE B. STEVEN	J. J. MURRAY

Some of Garrett's opponents apparently felt that their telegrams weren't nearly effective enough. One who expanded on his reasons, in letter form, was a local politician named George A. Knight:

Dallas, Texas
Dec. 13, 1901

The President,
Washington, D. C.

Sir:

Last evening I wired you that my information was that the appointment of Mr. Pat Garrett as Collector of Customs at El Paso,

Texas would reflect no credit on your administration, and asked that you hold the matter in abeyance until I could write you to-day.

There are two very good reasons in my judgement why this appointment should not be made. The first is, that to appoint any man to any important office who has made a record for himself as a "killer" would, in my judgement, seriously reflect on any administration.

I have not the pleasure of a personal acquaintance with Mr. Garrett, and presume that he has many good qualities, but I lived for years on the plains of Western Texas, near the New Mexico line, and know him quite well by reputation.

The second reason why this should not be made in my judgement is, that the appointment should go to some competent and worthy Texas Republican. Our party has heretofore been somewhat unfortunate in the appointment of Collectors at El Paso, and simply for the reason that they have not been generally the choice of the people, or the local Republicans, and consequently our local Organization out there has never been strengthened to any extent by the appointments that have been made there in the past.

I trust if this appointment has not been made when this reaches you, that you will give the matter your serious consideration with reference to the two objectives named.

In another communication enclosed herewith, I will make a recommendation for this appointment even at the risk of being thought presumptuous.

Very respectfully,

GEO. A. KNIGHT

Late Delegate to
Philadelphia Convention,
From 5th Congressional
District of Texas.

Pat Garrett at about the time that Theodore Roosevelt appointed him Collector of Customs for El Paso. (Courtesy of the University of Texas at El Paso Archives.)

Chapter 3

APPOINTMENT PENDING

Although Pat Garrett hadn't officially been appointed yet, the
El Paso *Herald* was reporting that he was in a front page article
of December 13, 1901:

VIEWS OF LOCAL MEN

On the Reported Appointment of Ex-Sheriff Pat Garrett.

SOME LOCAL MEN

Would Have Pleased the People Better, But Garrett Is
Highly Spoken Of As An Officer.

The expressions made today by local politicians and business men
on the report of Pat Garrett's appointment are of a widely different
character. There are many who feel that a local candidate should have
been selected by the President for the place.

In the past the office has always been considered the heritage of
Texas aspirants and this departure from the custom is causing adverse
comment among those who are not interested from a personal stand-
point. On the other hand there are some who say that the office is
as much the right of New Mexico as of any other part of the district.

To what political party Garrett belongs is one of the features discussed in all parts of the city today. It is doubted by no one that up
to three years ago he was a Democrat.

Since that time little can be learned except that he was elected
to the office of Sheriff of Dona Ana county through the support of
Republicans. Local Republicans say he accepted the office as a
Democrat, nevertheless, and was taken up by the Republicans solely
to secure his aid in the Fountain case.

Today numerous telegrams are being sent to the President requesting him to defer action until Texas can be heard from. The
dispatches are being signed by the business men of the city with but
few exceptions.

If the President consents to wait until a communication can reach him from this city it will be urged upon him that the appointment should be given to some of the candidates from the western end of the state.

These telegrams are not being sent in the interest of any one candidate but are simply the remonstrance of those who feel that an injustice will be done to the Republican party of this district if they are displaced by an outsider. There is no personal feeling against Garrett in the maneuver.

Friends of A. G. Foster, one of the candidates, today said that they were well satisfied with the situation. They received tips last night from friends in Washington that unless some action was taken today to cause the President to delay the name of Garrett would be sent to the Senate today. Since this has not been done it looks as if the requests from here for delay had taken hold.

What People Say.

A reporter called this morning on local people and asked them for an expression of what they thought about the appointment. Some refused for private reasons to be quoted and others spoke as follows:

H. B. Hamilton, formerly associate justice of the supreme court of New Mexico: "In some respects I think this is a good appointment as Garrett has always been considered a fine police officer. Until the last three years he has been considered a good Democrat. As a matter of local politics I feel that a local Republican ought to have been selected. It is my impression that this appointment is made in the interests of New Mexico politics. As a matter of fact this city has enough Republicans whose prominence and capabilities qualify them for office."

Was A Democrat.

W. W. Bridgers, attorney at law: "There is no doubt that Garrett was a Democrat when first Sheriff of Dona Ana county."

Garrett Switched.

J. S. Fielder, an attorney who has just arrived from Silver City: "He is a Republican now though he switched from the Democratic ranks about four years ago. I know him personally and he is a splendid fellow."

New Mexico is Entitled.

Judge Leigh Clark: "I think Garrett will make a good officer. He was a Democrat when first appointed Sheriff of Dona Ana County and subsequently became a Republican. I don't see why Texas has any more right to the appointment than New Mexico."

Good Appointment.

Judge John Franklin: "It is a very good appointment. I presume Texas people will object on the grounds that some Texas man should be given the place, but New Mexico is the largest part of the district and has a right to apply for the place. To the best of my knowledge Garrett is a Republican."

The Right Man.

A. A. Kline, heavy importer of Mexican goods: "I think Mr. Garrett will make a good officer. He is the right man in the right place. He will do his duty."

Still in the Race.

N. S. Corbin, one of the candidates for the office: "I am still in the fight and will be until the senate confirms the appointment of a collector for this port. I am not out of the race as has been reported and I want you to let my friends know it."

El Paso Has Suitable Men.

President Newman of the Lowdon bank: "This appointment is a surprise to me as well as to many others. From what I can learn Garrett is a good man and will make an efficient officer. El Paso is large enough to turn out a suitable man for the place, who would give as good satisfaction as an outsider."

Suits Him.

W. T. Hixson, jeweler: "The appointment suits me."

Has Enough Ability.

G. L. Newman, importer of cattle from Mexico: "Garrett is a man with enough ability to make a good collector."

Make a Good Collector.

A. Schwartz, importer of Mexican goods: "As far as I know Garrett will make a good collector. I had much rather see an El Paso man in the place. There are many here who could take better care of the place than an outsider."

Is Satisfied.

E. M. Fink, captain of customs inspectors: "Pat Garrett suits me. He has always been a good officer. I don't know about the office going to a local man, New Mexico comprises about three-fourths of the district."

Is Not Appointed.

N. Lapowski, one of the candidates: "I am satisfied that Garrett has not been appointed. I have not dropped out of the fight yet. All of the local men stand as much chance as they ever did."

President Knows Best.

Cashier Hilzinger of the International bank: "Garrett is a very good man for the place. I think that the President knows best what to do and if a local man was more eligible for the office he would have given him the place."

Uncle John.

John Julian: "I think an El Paso man should get it."

Missed a Chance.

Park Pitman, county clerk: "I believe Pat will make a good collector."
After expressing himself he quizzically gazed at the reporter and said in an almost inaudible voice: "I think Teddy could have done better by appointing me."

The same December 13, 1901, issue of the El Paso *Herald* also contained a related story about the Collector designate in the form of this biographical essay:

SKETCH OF GARRETT

Facts About the Reported New Collector.

HE IS AN OLD TIMER

In the Southwest, and Has Made a Reputation as a
Fearless Law Officer.

The career of Pat Garrett, who is reported to have been appointed by the President to the position of collector of customs for this port, is one filled with ups and downs. The greater part of his life has been spent in the cattle business. The most noteworthy event of his life is the killing of "Billy the Kid," a desperado who for a long time was a terror to the law abiding element of New Mexico.

In his time Garrett has seen many exciting events and taken a prominent part in them. On account of a courage that never faltered when duty called him to risk life in an undertaking he has often been successful where criminals were to be caught.

Garrett was born in Alabama in 1850 and when eight years of age left his home and came to Louisiana, where he remained until 1870. About this time he moved to Dallas county, Texas and engaged in farming.[1]

Eight years later he went with a party to the Buffalo range near Fort Griffin and spent about twelve months killing the buffalo which at that time were to be found in large droves. While on the range he had a number of thrilling experiences[2] and became, through his frequent hunting of bison, a crack shot.

Those were the days when the mighty buffalo were found in numbers that were seemingly inexhaustible. Day after day the slaughter was continued and yet no impression made on the herds that were being slowly wiped out to give way to cattle.

After this Garrett went to Fort Sumner in New Mexico and spent a year working on the cattle ranches in that vicinity. His next move was to Roswell where after six months on the ranges he moved to Lincoln county and was made a deputy sheriff under George Kimball. At the close of the latter's term Garrett was elected to succeed him and served for two years in the office of sheriff.[3]

He was a terror to bad men and established a reputation for ability in breaking up outlaw bands that have followed him ever since.

About this time the cattle rustlers were giving the ranchers a great deal of annoyance and to break up the gang Garrett was placed at the head of a company of fearless cowboys. Without killing

This Colt single action (serial number 55093) was taken from Billy Wilson by Pat Garrett when he captured the Kid and his gang at Stinking Springs in 1880. This is the gun that Garrett used to kill Billy the Kid on July 14, 1881, at Fort Sumner.

a single man the rustlers were forced to give up their depredations and the region was rid of the greatest scourge it has ever had. It took years to do this and mainly through the efforts of Garrett and his able assistants.[4]

An inducement from the Angus V. V. Ranch of Lincoln county, called Garrett back to New Mexico and he took charge of the ranch remaining there for several years. Owning a large tract of land on the Hondo river four miles below Roswell, he next went there and began to improve his holdings, building a home and acquiring a large number of cattle and fine horses.

Through the efforts of Garrett an irrigation ditch was built which takes its supply of water from the Hondo and distributes it over what was then an arid plain for miles around. To push the scheme a company was organized and in rapid succession others have followed until the entire valley is now fertile farms.[5]

This venture was in the spring of 1887. After making extensive improvements on his ranch Garrett sold out to an investment company which operated in the Pecos valley. With funds acquired from this source he moved to Uvalde, Texas and bought more land which he stocked and turned into a fine piece of property.

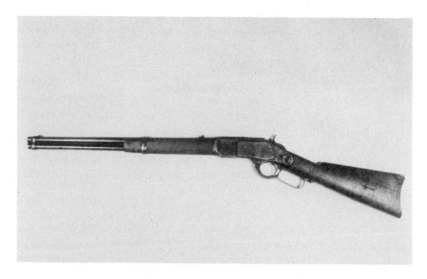

This 1873 Winchester carbine (serial number 47629) was also taken from Billy Wilson by Garrett. Garrett carried both the Colt and the Winchester throughout the remainder of his career as a lawman.

Since that time Garrett has been interested in mining and cattle raising. He owns a large ranch in the Organ mountains twenty-five miles east of Las Cruces, and several gold and turquoise claims in the Jarilla mountains. He has taken a prominent part in politics.

Mr. Garrett is a married man and his wife and five children reside at their ranch east of Roswell. In case the report of his intended appointment proves correct they will probably move to this city.

"Billy the Kid."

Pat Garrett's capture of "Billy the Kid" is one of the thrilling adventures of the southwest. With the death of this noted outlaw a band of border ruffians was broken up that long held the settlers in terror.

Having a pistol and knife in his hand, the Kid started to rapidly back off, at the same time raising his gun as if to shoot. Before he could pull the trigger Garrett shot him twice, the Kid falling to the floor dead. Garrett denies that more than two shots were fired by either of them.[6] In the same town the sheriff killed another of the gang.[7]

The death of the Kid caused those who were either in league or in sympathy with him to give up their preying on the respectable element.

Feels Thankful.

S. T. Gray, a cousin of the new collector, was in the city today and to a reporter for this paper said: "I am very proud to know that my cousin has secured this important position. Though we are only cousins I think as much of him as any member of the family. The president will have no cause to regret his action and the office will be well looked after."

By this time Pat Garrett was in Washington, staying at one of the District of Columbia's most posh hotels. It was at this address that Garrett received a batch of telegrams offering premature congratulations:

El Paso, Texas
December 13, 1901

P. F. Garrett
Care the Shoreham
Washington, D. C.

Accept our hearty congratulations.

GEO. OGDEN
NUMA G. BUCHOZ

El Paso, Texas
December 13, 1901

P. F. Garrett
Care the Shoreham
Washington, D. C.

Accept congratulations. Apparently all El Paso highly pleased excepting disappointed candidates. Advise Fall.

L. N. HIEL

El Paso, Texas
December 13, 1901

P. F. Garrett
Care The Shoreham,
Wash., D. C.

Teeth gnashing against your appointment being worked by opposition. If you want double amount signatures from business men than they sent wire.

L. N. HIEL AND FRIENDS

El Paso, Texas
December 13, 1901

P. F. Garrett
Care The Shoreham
Washn., D. C.

My congratulations. Every business and professional man in town highly pleased & all rejoicing excepting disappointed candidates and their friends.

L. W. EVANS

El Paso, Texas
December 13, 1901

Mr. Pat F. Garrett
Care The Shoreham,
Washington, D. C.

Smith and Stevens sending in protest and charges against you in the interest of Foster who is applicant.

R. F. CAMPBELL

Albuquerque, N. M.
December 13, 1901

P. F. Garrett
Care B. S. Rhodey,
House of Reps,
Washington, D. C.

Accept my heartiest congratulations on your appointment.

C. M. FORAKER

El Paso, Texas
Dec. 13, 1901

Pat F. Garrett
The Shoreham,
Washington, D. C.

Charles T. Marshall now in Washington wiring in here to get up charges against you.

R. F. CAMPBELL

Pat Garrett's mood was definitely upbeat, as is reflected in this letter he wrote to his wife, Apolinaria:

THE SHOREHAM

John T. Devine

Washington, D. C.
12-13th 1901

Dear Wife

I wired you yesterday (which I suppose you got) that I had been appointed Collector of Custombs (sic) at El Paso it will take 3 or 4 days to get Confirmed by the Senate and to make out bond and take Oath of office. Judge Fall and myself are doing all we can for Miss Mary. I may go by way of New Orleans to El Paso. if so will wire you to meet me at El Paso

The President paid me a great compliment when I went to see him one that any American would be very proud of I will tell you all

Mrs. Pat Garrett was photographed holding the Colt (serial number 55093) that killed Billy the Kid. This photograph was taken in 1933 after she successfully won her suit against the Tom Powers estate for the return of the gun that had been loaned to the Coney Island Saloon of El Paso by Pat Garrett in 1908. (Photo courtesy of Tom Kolberson.)

about it when I see you, which I hope will not be long it seems to me I love you and our babies bette (r) every

Yours

P. F. GARRETT

NOTES

1. Patrick Floyd Jarvis Garrett was born on June 5, 1850, in Chambers County, Alabama. He was the second of eight children born to John Lumpkin Garrett (1822-1868) and his wife Elizabeth Ann Jarvis (1829-1867). When Pat was three years old his father purchased the John Greer plantation in Claiborne Parish, Louisiana. The life of a gentleman farmer in the ante-bellum south may have been Pat Garrett's fate had not the Civil War come along to destroy that mint julep world forever.

Following the war, yankee carpetbaggers and scalawags moved in and confiscated most of the Garrett plantation's cotton crop. Financially ruined, Pat's father found solace in the bottle. Within a year both of Pat's parents died, leaving him a plantation that was more than $30,000 in the red. With nothing to remain for, Pat Garrett rode away from Louisiana on January 25, 1869, and headed west.

2. One of the "thrilling experiences" the *Herald* failed to mention was Garrett's killing of Joe Briscoe, a fellow buffalo hunter, during November, 1876. Garrett surrendered to the authorities at Fort Griffin, Texas, but they declined to prosecute.

3. On November 2, 1880, Pat Garrett was elected Sheriff of Lincoln County, New Mexico, having defeated his opponent, incumbent Sheriff George Kimball, by a vote of 320 to 179. Although Pat's term wouldn't officially begin until January 1, 1881, he was eager to capture Billy the Kid. In order to do this, Garrett had out-going Sheriff Kimball appoint him as a deputy for the remaining two months of Kimball's term. Garrett's manhunting was also aided by the fact that he held a Deputy U. S. Marshal's commission, allowing him to cross county lines.

4. This paragraph would seem to refer to Pat Garrett's brief stint as a Texas Ranger. On March 10, 1884, Governor John Ireland of Texas appointed Garrett a Lieutenant in the Texas Rangers. Within a year, Garrett resigned his commission, returning to his ranch near Roswell, New Mexico.

5. Pat Garrett discovered a great reservoir of artesian water in the Roswell region and went into partnership with two men to organize the Pecos Valley Irrigation and Investment Company on July 18, 1885. Garrett kept his irrigation scheme alive for several years. On January 15, 1887, he purchased a one-third interest in something called the Texas Ditch Company. The name proved prophetic when Garrett was "ditched" by his partners.

6. On the night of July 14, 1881, Sheriff Pat Garrett, accompanied by John William Poe (1850-1923) and Thomas L. "Tip" McKinney, approached the residence of Pedro Menard "Pete" Maxwell (1848-1898) in Fort Sumner, New Mexico. While Poe and McKinney waited outside,

Garrett went into an unlighted bedroom to awaken the sleeping Maxwell. Within seconds after Garrett entered the room, the Kid appeared and spotted Poe and McKinney.

"Quien Es?" the Kid called out in Spanish. When he received no reply, the Kid drew a six-shooter from the waistband of his trousers and began backing into the bedroom that Garrett had entered only moments before.

Once inside the dark room the Kid asked Maxwell in Spanish: "Pete, who are those fellows on the outside?"

Suddenly, the Kid was aware of another person, besides Maxwell and himself, being in the room. Once again he hissed "Quien Es?" Sheriff Garrett recognized the voice and shot twice—his first shot killing the Kid instantly and the second missing.

Ironically, the Kid's repeated question, "Quien Es?" (Who is it?), was never answered, and he died without knowing that he had been done in by a one-time drinking buddy named Pat Garrett.

7. On December 19, 1880, Billy the Kid, Dave Rudabaugh, Billy Wilson, Charlie Bowdre, Tom Pickett and Tom O'Folliard rode into Fort Sumner. Awaiting them was a posse led by Pat Garrett, who opened fire killing O'Folliard. The Kid and his companions managed to escape unharmed.

*Pat Garrett (right) with his brother, Alfred, in about 1900.
(Courtesy of Jarvis P. Garrett.)*

Chapter 4

APPOINTMENT SENT
TO SENATE

Despite the hoopla, and nagging by Albert B. Fall, President Roosevelt still wanted a little more time to consider Garrett's appointment before sending his name to the Senate for confirmation. The El Paso *Herald* reported the situation on page one of their issue of December 14, 1901:

VIEW FROM THE CAPITAL

Of the Contest Now Being Waged Over Collectorship

GARRETT'S NAME

May Yet Be Sent To the Senate, So the
Report Comes From Washington.

HAWLEY'S NOMINEE

Was Waller Burns, and He Thought He Was Surely
In Line For the Place.

Vigorous Protests Being Made Against Garrett
On Political Grounds and Alleged
Personal Unfitness.

WASHINGTON, Dec. 14.—The decision of the President to nominate Garrett as collector of customs at El Paso has caused vigorous opposition from Texas. Ex-Representative Hawley, Republican national committeeman of Texas, is in Cuba. He cannot conduct the fight, but the Republican leaders in Texas are doing all the execution possible to Garrett by means of telegrams.

They represent that Garrett is unfit for the place and that his nomination would be a serious reflection on the character of the Republican organization in Texas. The Texans declare there is plenty of material in Texas to fill this office, without having to take a man who has no superior qualifications.

Hawley recommends State Senator Waller D. Burns for the collectorship and has believed that the appointment would be made.

It is declared that the Republican organization of Texas is unlike that in other Southern states, being harmonious and composed of a good class of men. The President had not consulted the organization in some of the southern states about filling of offices, but it was expected by the Texans that their organization would be recognized.

If the nomination of Garrett is suspended long enough, the Republican national committee will likely take a hand in sustaining the organization of Texas in its contention.

Miss Strong, Hawley's secretary, was at the White House today and yesterday, bearing many protests.

A. B. Fall and John Hart have seen the President. The President refused to discuss the question today. According to the present outlook the nomination of Garrett will be sent to the Senate Monday, or Tuesday at the latest.

With the realization that his appointment still had a chance of falling through, Garrett asked his friends to send off another batch of endorsements. Once again, the White House telegrapher must have wished he called in sick. Here are a few examples of the pro-Garrett messages:

El Paso, Tex.
Dec. 14

The President:

We believe Pat Garrett would make a good and efficient collector. His record is clean. We endorse his application.

The International
Exchange Bank.

El Paso, Texas
Dec. 14, 1901

The President:

Recommended Foster for fitness and asked delay to have him considered, but attack on Pat Garrett wholly unwarranted; not a gambler. Have known him many years. Record clean.

J. M. HAWKINS

Managing Editor, News

El Paso, Texas
December 14.

President Roosevelt:

Garrett stands well in this country and if made collector at this place we think he will fill the office with credit to all concerned. We consider him honest and competent.

B. F. HAMMETT,

Mayor.

El Paso, Texas
December 14.

His Excellency,
The President:

While Neff is our first choice, we take pleasure in saying we believe Garrett would make honest and efficient collector this port. He is not a gambler and know nothing derogatory his moral character.

H. L. NEWMAN

President,
Lowden National Bank

El Paso, Texas
December 14.

Secretary of The Treasury:

I cordially endorse Garrett for collector of customs. He is well thought of by the business men of this city.

S. J. FRENDENTHALL

El Paso, Texas
December 14, 1901

Theo. Roosevelt, President:

While I endorse and urge Neff's candidacy for collector and believe him above all others entitled and qualified because of being republican, for services during Civil War, and his having never held government office, through qualification and honesty and possessing confidence and good will of entire community, I must subscribe to Garrett's qualifications and great service to the Southwest as her officer.

J. A. EDDY

Beaumont, Texas
Dec. 14, 1901.

Hon. Theodore Roosevelt:

Consider Garrett's selection wise and good. Is capable, honest and worthy. Will write you fully from Abilene.

JAMES G. LOWDON

Of course, there has to be a sour apple in every barrel, and amidst the pile of Garrett endorsements was included this lone squeak of protest from a vacationing Texan:

Jacksonville, Fla.,
Dec. 14, 1901.

The President:

Referring case Mr. Garrett, New Mexico, am informed he defaulted in sum of three thousand dollars; suit to recover now pending Donohue County; have sent for certified copy record. Please hold appoint.

CECIL A. LYONS

Chairman
Texas Republican Committee.

As added insurance, Garrett gave several of the telegrams of congratulations he received on December 13 to his friend B. S. Rodey, along with this letter:

Washington, D. C.

Hon. B. S. Rodey,
M. C. New Mexico,
Washington, D. C.

Sir:

I herewith hand you a few unsolicited telegrams from Texas, bearing on the matter of my appointment as Collector at El Paso.

Those of Postmaster Campbell and Editor Hawkins, showing source and meaning of opposition, in conjunction with the others, should it seems to me be a sufficient answer to charges and protests made against me.

I thank you for your recommendation, and assure you that my conduct of the office will reflect credit upon my endorsers.

I have endorsed each telegram showing who the sender is. You are at liberty to use these as to you may seem best.

Very truly yours,

P. F. GARRETT

Rodey lost no time getting Garrett's letter, and the telegrams of endorsement, to the place they would do the most good:

Washington, D. C.
December 14, 1901

Hon. G. B. Cortelyou,
Secretary to the President.

Sir:

Referring to letter of Mr. Garrett, enclosed, you will find some of the telegrams selected by me, and considering that some objection has been made to Mr. Garrett, as you know, I would like to have you, if you think best, call the President's attention to the same, particularly as they come from El Paso and not from New Mexico.

With assurances of my highest regards, I am,

Sincerely yours,

B. S. RODEY

Del. from N. M.

Finally, it became official. As usual, it was the El Paso *Herald* that got the scoop in their front page article of December 16, 1901:

GARRETT'S NAME

Sent To the Senate Today
By President Roosevelt

Special to the Herald.

WASHINGTON, D. C., Dec. 16.—The nomination of Patrick F. Garrett to be collector of customs at El Paso was sent to the senate today by the President.

Garrett will unquestionably be confirmed.

President Roosevelt is much pleased with Garrett's record and personality.

Special to the Herald.

SANTA FE, N. M., Dec. 16.—Garrett's nomination is satisfactory to the Republicans in this territory as far as recognition of New Mexico is concerned, but as Garrett was considered an anti-administration man his appointment is not especially pleasing to the Otero Republicans, who, however, when they saw his good show for appointment fell over themselves to endorse him.

Garrett's appointment means that New Mexico has the same claim upon Roosevelt as a territory as it would as a state.

A leading El Paso Republican voices the local sentiment as follows:

"I think that the President has made a serious mistake in not waiting for the return of National Committeeman Hawley before

Henry McCarty, alias Billy the Kid as he appeared in about 1880.

A letter from Pat Garrett to his wife, Apolinaria, that was written on December 13, 1901. (Courtesy of Craig A. Fouts of Encinitas, CA.)

making this appointment so that Texas could have been heard from in the matter through her national representative. If this office is by right a New Mexico appointment it could have been determined after hearing from both sides. As it is, I believe it will have a bad effect on our local and state politics."

The sending of the name of Pat Garrett to the Senate for confirmation to the office of collector of this port is exciting a great deal of comment among the Republicans of this city who have for several years stood by their guns and fought against odds.

On every hand it can be heard that an injustice has been done local party leaders. The failure of the President to pay heed to the numerous telegrams asking that action be deferred until Texas could be heard from is creating a great deal of surprise as it was supposed that he would not refuse to listen to what they might have to say in regard of one of the most important federal offices within his gift for this district.

For the past two days it has been confidently hoped that no action would be taken until after the holidays, and if reports be

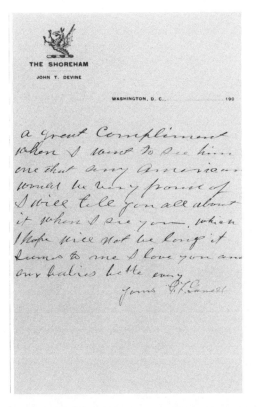

correct the president has given out information that has caused this impression to become general.

No reason for his haste in the matter is assigned and why he changed his mind and sent the name of Garrett to the Senate at this time is a matter of conjecture.

There is no disposition on the part of leading Republicans seen this afternoon to give up the fight for establishing the party on a firm basis in this section of the country.

While feeling is strong against the appointment of Garrett on political and not personal grounds, his election will serve to make the party here even more strongly united than ever before.

"We are not satisfied with this appointment," said a prominent Republican this afternoon, "though it is not on personal grounds. The office belongs to a local man and the failure of the President to appoint one will meet with disfavor among those who have the best interests of the city at heart.

"They can all talk about the best man for the place but that does not overcome the fact that each locality is entitled to a certain amount of patronage and this office by every right belongs to El Paso.

"There is any number of capable men in this end of the state who could take charge of the office and conduct it with as much credit as any outsider.

"I do not think this passing by of local timber will give the impression that we are without good men here, but it does look as if the President had no desire to consider what the Republicans here have done in the past and will continue to do in the future."

Garrett is expected to arrive in the city shortly. It was reported yesterday that he was on his way to Las Cruces and would probably not stop there but come to this city.

Already several letters have come to the collector's office addressed to "Hon. Patrick Garrett, collector of customs, port of El Paso."

It might be added that none of them are from Washington but are postmarked at different places in Texas.

Another note of tension was added by the U. S. Senate—which decided to take their holiday hiatus before acting on Garrett's nomination. The El Paso *Herald* of Thursday, December 19, 1901, was confident that the delay wouldn't present any real problem and said as much in this front page story:

GARRETT'S NOMINATION NOT YET ACTED UPON

Senate Adjourns Without Taking Up the Matter,
Which Now Goes Over Until January 6.

Special to The Herald.

WASHINGTON, Dec. 19—The Senate has not yet confirmed Garrett's nomination.

The Senate adjourned today until January 6. The nomination will be taken up then.

Charges against Garrett were filed before the committee on finance, alleging gambling. Garrett replied to Representative Spooner of the Committee that he did not know the difference between a straight flush and four of a kind.

Other charges were made by the opposition. Senator Hanna is opposed to confirmation. The nomination will be confirmed almost unquestionably when the revenue offices are taken up.

A recently discovered photograph that is believed to be that of Billy the Kid. (Copyrighted by Creative Publishing Co.)

Theodore Roosevelt in 1912. This photograph, taken by Charles Duprez, has been reproduced more times than any other Roosevelt photograph. (Jack DeMattos Collection.)

Chapter 5

CONFIRMATION AS COLLECTOR OF CUSTOMS

Pat Garrett arrived in El Paso on Christmas Day, spending what was probably the most joyous holiday season of his entire life surrounded by friends and family. A complete report of Pat's triumphful return was given by the El Paso *Herald* in their issue of December 26, 1901:

GARRETT IS HERE

The New Collector Not Ready To Take Hold Just Yet.

OTHER PILGRIMS

Tell Of Their Experiences in Washington, and
Interviews With President Roosevelt.

After resting from the tiring effects of his trip from Washington to this city, Pat Garrett, the recently appointed collector of customs for this port, consented this afternoon to talk for publication.

Collector Garrett arrived in the city last night over the Texas & Pacific railroad and was met at the depot by a number of his friends in this city. He at once went to the Grand Central hotel where Mrs. Garrett and children were awaiting his return. Tonight they will leave over the Santa Fe for Las Cruces.

"I am not prepared to say when I will take charge of the office," said Collector Garrett this morning. "It will probably be in a few days, and on my return from New Mexico I will be in a position to give out more definite information.

"In regard to the appointment of deputies which will be about the first move made after I assume active charge of the office, I am not prepared to say. The fact is I have not decided whom to place in the positions.

"I went to Washington for the purpose of getting this place though the fight I made was not very active. I laid the matter before the President and then waited for results.

"For the people of this city I have the kindest of feelings and am certain that I have many friends here who are to be depended upon when they are needed to help me. The fight for this office has been fair and above board and I was fortunate enough to win out.

"The policy of the office will be to conduct it along lines that are legitimate and that will result to the credit of the administration. At this time I know of no changes that will be made in the system already adopted. The office is here for a purpose and that purpose will be carried out.

"In regard to the charges made against me at Washington I want to say that the President considered the source from which they came more than he did the charges themselves. They had no weight whatever with the President in his action in this matter.

"I cannot say whether or not I will make this city my residence in the future. At the present time I am a resident of New Mexico and it is likely that I will continue as such.

"The district this office covers is made up almost entirely of New Mexico and I think the patronage belongs there more than any other place. It is no hardship upon Texas to have the place go to someone outside of El Paso.

"I owe my appointment in a large measure to Judge Fall of this city. He rendered me considerable valuable assistance and I owe him a debt of gratitude. I guess the President wanted me to have the place and that is why I got it.

"About the last remark President Roosevelt made when we parted was, "Mr. Garrett, I am betting on you," and I replied, "Mr. President you will win that bet." That was just before I left him to start for Texas.

"I consider President Roosevelt to be the greatest man this country has ever had. When I met him in Washington it was for the first time. We were not personally acquainted prior to my introduction to him in Washington.

"I do not care to talk about New Mexico politics at this time. I feel that it would not be good policy for me to express an opinion while things are not settled.

"This morning I received an official letter from the Secretary of the Treasury informing me that my commission had been made out and would be forwarded to me in short time. My bond of twenty-five thousand dollars was secured in Washington through a surety company though I had offers from private parties of six times that amount."

Collector Garrett was asked to talk about the capture of "Billy the Kid," and replied that the less said about that affair the better he liked it. He has written an account of the Kid's ending and when asked where the book could be found refused to give the information. The new collector if he has his way will bury the event.

Judge Fall Talks.

While Garrett was being interviewed Judge Fall stood by and offered suggestions that helped the former in answering questions put to him. (author's italics)

Later Judge Fall was asked about the charge of misappropriation of funds while Garrett was Sheriff of Dona Ana county, New Mexico, and replied:

"The county owed Garrett about four thousand dollars for money he had expended in the discharge of his duties. Later he made a collection of three thousand dollars of the county money and, as his attorney, I advised him to keep it. Then I went to the district attorney and asked him to make a charge against Garrett that the matter might be settled up.

"This was done and the result was that Garrett was allowed to keep the money and the county commissioners ordered that the remainder be paid to him. To do this a special tax has been levied and as soon as it is collected he will be paid about eight hundred dollars which is due him.

"There was no breaking of the law on Garrett's part as the money was his legitimately and he took that means of collecting it. His action was sustained by the courts, and a settlement made of the matter.

"Pat Garrett has been appointed to this place because of his record and ability. The President found him to be competent and had no confidence in the charges made against him from this section of the district."

Alderman Baum's Views.

Alderman Baum was seen in his office this morning and talked about things which took place in Washington while he was there. Mr. Baum returned to the city last Tuesday after an abscence of two weeks in Washington. He was there looking after his interests, being a candidate for the collectorship.

"I met the President in Washington and talked to him about the office," says Mr. Baum. "He referred the matter to the Secretary of the Treasury and promised that all applications would be considered by that member of the cabinet. This was before the telegrams reached him.

"The effect of the numerous telegrams sent from this city to the President was to cause the withholding of the appointment from the Senate for four days. I suppose the President during that time was thinking the matter over.

"I am reliably informed that this is the effect the dispatches had.

I learned that they were arriving through the Texas organization and that there were telegrams sent to the President to counteract the effect of those sent in opposition to Garrett.

"When I reached Washington it looked as if an El Paso man would get the place, and it continued to look that way up to the time Lew Wallace called on the President. He recommended Garrett highly for the position. The President told Garrett one week ago last Wednesday that he would in all probability appoint him.

"There was no personal feeling among the candidates gathered at Washington. We met daily at the hotel and talked the situation over with each other. Each was making his own fight and making it his own way.

"We would like to have seen the Texas organization heard in this matter before the appointment was made. The general feeling throughout Texas, as shown by the telegrams received in Washington from all over the state, was that a home man should have the place.

"While away I attended two sessions of Congress and heard some eloquent appeals on the measures before that body. It is my impression that the Senate at this session of Congress is a fine body of men, who will look after the country's interests. They have hardly got down to business yet. The Texas delegation is strong and able."

It was ironic that Garrett's fate as Collector of Customs shared the same front page of that particular El Paso *Herald* of December 26, 1901, with a related item concerning another Roosevelt appointment. This particular appointee was about to become Garrett's boss:

SHAW HAS ACCEPTED TREASURY PORTFOLIO

He Is Recognized As Authority On Banking and Finance.

WASHINGTON, Dec. 26—It is announced from the White House that Governor Shaw accepts the portfolio of the Treasury department and will succeed Secretary Gage next week. He will fill out his term as governor of Iowa which ends Thursday evening, and then proceed direct to Washington.

The President agrees to retain in office Secretary Wilson of Iowa, such being entirely in harmony with his desires. Governor Shaw made this request.

Governor Shaw is recognized authority on banking and currency matters and is a practical banker. His appointment will please all the west and is a shrewd political stroke.[1]

The following day, December 27, 1901, the El Paso *Herald* reported that Pat Garrett was appointing an old friend from New Mexico as his assistant:

BUCHOZ WILL BE DEPUTY

Garrett Has Gone Back To Las Cruces, and Will Return the First Of the Year.

Collector Garrett and family left last night for Las Cruces, where he will remain until about the first of the year. Upon his return friends in this city will hold a banquet in his honor at the Zelger at which forty guests will be present.

Numa Buchoz will be given the position of deputy collector. Those to fill the other positions will be announced later. Mr. Buchoz held an official position in Dona Ana county, New Mexico, when Garrett was sheriff for the first time. They formed a friendship then which has resulted in securing for the New Mexican the position of deputy.

Collector Garrett spent yesterday visiting friends in the city and receiving congratulations. He called at the federal building and took a look around the office he will soon occupy. It is probable that he will assume charge on the first of the year.

When the Senate reconvened on January 6, 1902, their first order of business was Pat Garrett's confirmation. There were no objections and the Committee on Finance quickly waved the nomination through. With his appointment finally official, Garrett's forty supporters gathered at the Zelger and treated him to a banquet. During the event, the toastmaster (probably Albert B. Fall) supposedly remarked: "Here is the man that President Roosevelt was worried about, because he had the reputation of being a poker player. Everybody in El Paso knows that Pat Garrett isn't a poker player. He only THINKS he's a poker player."[2]

NOTES

1. Leslie Mortier Shaw was born in Morristown, Vermont, on November 2, 1848. He worked his way through Cornell College and went on to get his law degree from the Iowa College of Law in 1876. On December 6, 1877, Shaw married Alice Cranshaw by whom he had three children.

Shaw subsequently made a fortune in banking. His political career began when he replied to William Jennings Bryan's "Cross of Gold" speech in 1896. As a result, Shaw was nominated for Governor of Iowa in 1898. He was elected and served two terms.

In 1900 Shaw campaigned for Theodore Roosevelt as Vice President. When T. R. was elevated to the Presidency he appointed Shaw his Secretary of the Treasury in 1902. Although his ultra-protectionist views often exasperated Roosevelt, the President retained him even after Shaw offered to resign in 1905. He remained as Secretary of the Treasury until March, 1907.

Shaw went on to have a distinguished banking career as head of the Carnegie Trust Company and later the First Mortgage Guarantee & Trust Company of Philadelphia. In addition, he wrote two books and remained politically active right up to his death at eighty-three on March 28, 1932.

2. While this is a well-known quote concerning Garrett, there doesn't seem to be any *contemporary* record of it. The earliest source that this writer has found is William A. Keleher's 1945 book, *The Fabulous Frontier*, (Rydal Press, Santa Fe, New Mexico). On page 72 of that work Keleher wrote:

"Roosevelt had a weakness for appointing gunmen and western characters to important administrative positions. He knew about Pat Garrett's brush with "Billy the Kid," and that among his other qualifications, he was handy with a six-shooter. The President was a bit disturbed by the flood of telegrams that reached him, protesting against Garrett's appointment because he was a race horse follower and a poker player. Confirmed as Collector of the Customs in 1901, the people of El Paso gave a banquet in Pat Garrett's honor. Introducing Garrett, the toastmaster said . . ." And, at that point Keleher gave the quote we have reprinted in chapter five. For the purposes of this work, Keleher's wording of the quote has been used. Subsequent usage of the quote, by writers after Keleher, managed to keep the essential message intact but switched a word of phrase around.

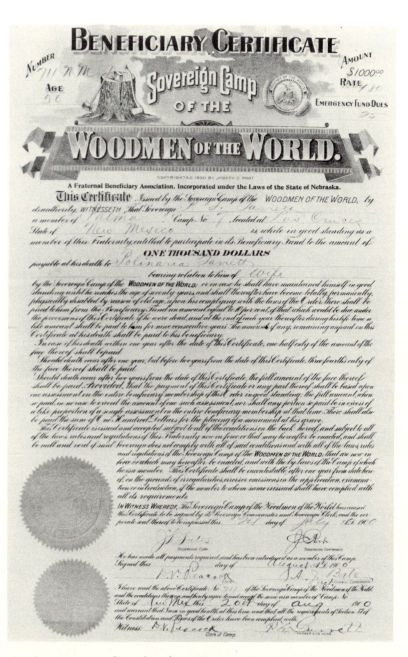

An insurance policy for $1,000 that Pat Garrett took out on August 20, 1900 which named his wife, Apolinaria, as the beneficiary. (Courtesy of Craig A. Fouts, Encinitas, CA.)

Pat Garrett (right) with his brother, Hillary, in El Paso in about 1900. (Courtesy of Jarvis P. Garrett.)

Chapter 6

EARLY PROBLEMS

One of the first incidents that caused Garrett's supporters some concern came when J. D. Campbell of the Corralitos Ranch near Casas Grandes, Mexico, shipped four separate herds of young cattle, totaling more than 3,000 head, across the Rio Grande to El Paso.

The appraising of cattle was one of the chief duties of the El Paso Customs House. Normally a collector would appoint a specialist in the field to carry out this task; but since Garrett (who had worked with livestock for most of his life) considered himself an expert, he carried out this particular function himself.

When the Corralitos Ranch shipped their four herds to El Paso, they described them all as calves. Collector Garrett disagreed and claimed that more than half were more than one year old—meaning that the owners had to pay a higher duty of $3.75 per head as opposed to the $2.00 per head for calves.

J. D. Campbell protested Garrett's decision to the Board of Appraisers in New York—but months would pass before the matter was resolved. Finally, on August 22, 1902, the board handed down a decision that only 587 head were more than one year old—which was almost 1,300 less than the number Garrett quoted.

Pat promptly appealed the decision, vowing to go as far as the Supreme Court if necessary. He only got as far as the U. S. Circuit Court, which dismissed the case.

The first of many times that Collector Garrett and his boss, Secretary of the Treasury Leslie M. Shaw, locked horns came during this period. This time the issue was not the appraisal of cattle—but "bona fide tourists." Garrett's views in the matter were supported by the El Paso *Times* who gave this report in their issue of August 27, 1902:

SHAW SETTLES DUTY QUESTION

Hereafter All Tourists from Mexico Will Be Allowed to Bring Into the U. S. $100 Worth of Goods.

MUST BE FOR OWN USE

Bona Fide Tourists Can Bring In Anything They Please If It Is For Their Own Personal Use.

Secretary Shaw, in reply to a letter addressed to him by Collector Garrett asking for a direct opinion on the much mooted "$100 duty free personal effect" question, has referred the collector to a circular issued in May by the department bearing on that subject and instructing him to be governed by that circular.

The result is that any bona fide tourist can bring in free of duty $100 worth of goods provided they are intended for his own personal use. He cannot bring them in unless he intends to use them.

"All we can do," said the collector, "is to be sure that the passenger who brings the article in is a genuine tourist. Of course, we will not permit people to go over to Juarez and come back with $100 worth of goods unless they are really tourists. But there is nothing to prevent a person residing here from going to Chihuahua, for instance, and coming back with whatever he chooses to bring if such articles are for his personal use.

"Our force is not large enough to keep watch on all those bringing in things under the new ruling to see that they really use them themselves, but if we get evidence to the effect that the goods are disposed of to others we can treat the cases as we do those of smuggling."

Mr. Garrett seems to think the ruling is going to cause much trouble here, as it will bring up so many problems as to what articles can properly be claimed by a tourist as being for personal use.

It is the opinion of many that the ruling is really a bit of favoritism shown European travelers who annually go from the United States to points abroad and bring back relics and other souvenirs which they have heretofore been unable to pass duty with. The ruling will, no doubt, originate an illegitimate trade at ports like El Paso that will be hard to suppress.

In the meantime, Secretary Shaw was receiving a stack of letters that were critical of Garrett. Then, during February, 1903, I. A. Barnes, an American businessman working out of Juarez, Mexico, circulated a petition calling for Garrett's removal. Unintended comedy developed when Barnes suggested himself as the ideal replacement for Garrett. The El Paso papers laughed the entire incident off by claiming that Barnes' petition had "received the merry ha ha and the cold shoulder."[1]

Nonetheless, Barnes' petition had the desired effect on Secretary of the Treasury Leslie M. Shaw who sent Garrett a reprimand that instructed him to practice politeness on the job. Shaw's rebuke so humiliated Garrett, that he—supposedly—went over his superior's head and wrote the President directly.

In a letter of February 8, 1903, Garrett complained: "It has been my ambition to treat all persons doing business with this office with the upmost courtesy, and if in any case it has not been done I certainly did not know of it."[2]

Secretary Shaw responded by sending Joseph F. Evans to check up on Garrett's performance. Evans asked Garrett to appoint George M. Gaither to do the cattle inspecting. Garrett objected but a compromise solution was reached when it was decided to appoint Gaither for a thirty-day "trial period" commencing on March 9, 1903.

Only two days after Gaither's appointment, the Houston *Post* brought its readers up to date on Garrett's problems in its issue of March 11, 1903:

CHARGES AGAINST GARRETT

Are Based on Alleged Lack of Courtesy and Politeness.

WASHINGTON, March 10—For several days past rumors have been going the rounds here to the effect that charges of a serious nature had been made against Patrick F. Garrett, collector of customs at El Paso, and that his removal was probable.

Similar stories seem to have been told in Texas for several applications for the prospective vacancy have been received by the Treasury

Department. The names of these applicants have not been divulged, inasmuch as the position for which they are applying is not vacant.

It appears that a number of complaints have been filed against Garrett, most of which have had reference to the general conduct of his office.

A conspicuous absence of tact and common politeness on his part seems to have been the principal feature on which most of the complaints were based. In several of them it is said that gruffness and lack of courtesy were specifically mentioned.

Secretary Shaw took cognizance of the complaints to the extent of writing Garrett a letter advising him to make some experiments in the line of being polite and courteous to those compelled to do business with his office. The letter did not contain this literal language, but that was the effect of it.

The Treasury Department now considers the incident as entirely closed. Assistant Secretary Armstrong so informed the *Post* correspondent today.

Garrett, it will be remembered, was appointed in the face of protests from all the Republican leaders and dozens of the rank and file in Texas.

He came to Washington without any thought of getting an office. The President heard that he was the slayer of the outlaw known as "Billy the Kid," and that, to use the President's own language, he was "middlin' handy with a gun." Therefore he was appointed to the collectorship.

This is not the first time his conduct of the office has been called to the attention of the treasury department. Only a few weeks ago complaint was made of his alleged arbitrary actions with reference to the collections of the duty on a bunch of cattle brought over from Mexico. The department paid only passing attention to the complaints filed at the time.

Among those who read the account in the Houston *Post* was a former Texas Ranger who sent a letter supporting Garrett to President Roosevelt:

Arnim, Texas
Mch. 12th 1903

Hon. Theodore Roosevelt,
Washington, D. C.

Sir,

I find in Houston *Post* of yesterday, clipping enclosed, a statement concerning Mr. P. F. Garrett of El Paso, Tex. I was for some time a private in Co. D, Texas Rangers with headquarters at a little town called Ysleta just twelve miles south of El Paso.

I was in the Collector's office a "few weeks" since when this complainant entered and can say that the clerk treated him very courteously.

I think the real truth of the case is that Mr. Garrett tries to attend to the duties of his office according to the law and that don't please some of the "rich people" who seem to think they ought to be given a discount in paying duties.

I am in no way concerned in the case and only like to see "fair play" and don't like to see anyone abused and talked about simply for trying to do his duty.

With best wishes,

Respectfully,

H. E. DELANY

NOTES

1. This unidentified newspaper quote was cited by Leon C. Metz in his book *Pat Garrett: The Story of a Western Lawman*, pp. 246-247.

2. The source for this letter from Garrett to Roosevelt, is the 1964 reprint of Pat Garrett's *Authentic Life of Billy the Kid*, published by Horn and Wallace of Albuquerque. The letter was quoted in an introduction for the book written by Pat's son, Jarvis P. Garrett.

Pat Garrett may not have enjoyed quite as intimate a relationship with the President as Bat Masterson and Ben Daniels. Apparently, whatever relationship they may have had didn't extend to regular correspondence. In any event, this letter from Garrett to Roosevelt remains, at this time, the only known written communication that may have passed between the two men.

Six-foot-five-inch Pat Garrett was photographed at Teddy Roosevelt's Rough Rider reunion in San Antonio in 1905. (Courtesy of Leon Metz.)

Chapter 7

FISTICUFFS IN THE STREET

When the unwanted George M. Gaither's thirty-day "trial period" of employment was up, Collector Garrett lost no time in writing his boss this note:

CUSTOMS SERVICE

OFFICE OF THE COLLECTOR

El Paso, Texas.,
April 7, 1903

The honorable Secretary of
the Treasury,
Washington, D. C.

Sir:

I have the honor to enclose herewith the oath of office of Mr. George M. Gaither, appointed temporary inspector on March 9, 1903, for a period of thirty days at the compensation of $3.00 per diem.

The opinions of the Special Agent at this port and myself, have been at variance regarding the values placed on Mexican cattle imported at this port, and after consultation it was agreed to appoint some disinterested person for a limited time, to inquire, and ascertain if possible, the situation of the cattle markets in Mexico looking toward a closer agreement between the two offices upon the question involved.

Mr. Gaither was selected by the Special Agent as the proper person to secure this information, and as his term of office expires to day, and his services of no further material value for the purpose for which he was appointed, I respectfully request my action be approved and authority be granted to pay him.

Respectfully,

PATRICK F. GARRETT

Collector of Customs.

When Garrett handed Gaither his walking papers, the latter asked why he had not been reappointed. Pat's reply was that he had no authority to employ Gaither full time. With this news, Gaither stormed off. Soon Garrett began hearing rumors that Gaither was complaining that Pat had promised him a permanent position. Bad blood was up and the inevitable confrontation wasn't long in coming. The first report of the clash was contained in the Friday, May 8, 1903, issue of the El Paso *Herald:*

U. S. OFFICIALS SCRAP

Collector Garrett and Ex-Cattle Appraiser Gaither
Have A Fisticuff on San Antonio Street

This morning about eleven o'clock Customs Collector Pat Garrett and former special cattle appraiser Geo. Gaither, of the customs department, met on the side walk in front of the Nations Meat Market on San Antonio Street when a dispute arose which resulted in a fist fight.

Jim Biggs of the Nations Market, and Policeman Gonzales rushed in and separated the men before any serious damage was done. They were both placed under arrest on a charge of fighting and gave bond. They will be tried before Recorder Eylar this afternoon or tomorrow.

After the trouble a *Herald* man asked Mr. Garrett how it started and he said:

"About sixty days ago I engaged Mr. Gaither to look into the matter of cattle appraisements at this port and told him that when he was through that would be all the work there was for him and that the job would be for about thirty days.

"When the thirty days were up I let him out and since then he has said that I promised him a regular position and failed to keep my word. I met him this morning and asked him about it and a fight resulted."

The reporters were unable to find Mr. Gaither for a statement.

A more detailed account of the Garrett-Gaither donnybrook was given later that day in the May 8, 1903, issue of the El Paso *Evening News:*

HAVE A FIGHT

Collector of the Port Pat Garrett and George M. Gaither
Come to Blows.

NO HARM WAS DONE

Friends Separated the Combatants While They Were Fighting
All Over the Sidewalk on San Antonio Street.

INVESTIGATION BEING HELD

Collector Garrett Admits That Cattle Appraisement
Is Being Looked Into by Treasury.

Port Collector of Customs Patrick F. Garrett and George M. Gaither, who was appointed some time ago as special appraiser of cattle here, had a little fisticuff on San Antonio Street shortly after 10:30 o'clock this morning, in front of the Nations Meat Market.

It appears that there has been bad feeling between the two men for some time because of the appraiser's dismissal from government service.

The two men met accidentally and Mr. Gaither accused Collector Garrett of acting towards him in bad faith. He said that Chief Deputy Numa Buchoz had promised him the job permanently, speaking for the collector, and he thought he should have it.

One word led to another and Collector Garrett called Gaither a liar. At this Mr. Gaither hauled off and a lively mix-up ensued. Quite a number of blows were exchanged.

The fight was progressing in rapid fashion when County Attorney Maury Kemp rushed in to separate them. He grabbed Mr. Gaither around the waist and tried to pull him off. Former Policeman James Biggs came out of the Nations' Meat Market and also began separating the contestants.

This photograph taken at the Rough Rider reunion in 1905 shows Roosevelt (third from left), Garrett (fourth from right), and Tom Powers (third from right.) (Courtesy of Leon Metz.)

Maury Kemp was backed up against an iron door of the meat shop and his back was hurt.

Captain Garrett got in a few telling parting blows as the clinch was stopped and his diamond ring cut Gaither on the face. Gaither says that Garrett got excited and scratched him; that he was worse to fight than a catamount.

The fight was more or less ludicrous. It was a fist fight pure and simple, as neither of the contestants was armed.

Some twenty-five men were all trying to separate the scrappers at once and the scene was bordering on the comic opera style for a few moments.

Chief of Police Peyton J. Edwards arrested both men and they were released on their own recognizance to appear before the court this evening.

Collector Garrett was seen this morning. He said:

"The whole trouble came up about the appointment. Gaither claimed that he should be made an appraiser of cattle. Colonel Evans had him appointed and I kept him on for thirty days, until I thought I had no further use for his services.

A second photograph taken at the Rough Rider reunion shows Garrett (second from left) next to President Roosevelt. Tom Powers is second from the right. (Courtesy of Leon Metz.)

"I have no authority to appoint such a man. That is vested in the Secretary of the Treasury, and I told Gaither that when we met this morning.

"I guess the fight was more or less funny, as neither one of us are much as pugilists.

"Gaither is a chronic disturber. He is trying to butt into the government service whether he is wanted or not. He told someone a few days ago to file an application for my job, as it would not be long before I would be discharged."

Investigation Being Held.

Collector Garrett was asked whether he knew that an investigation of the appraisement of cattle had been ordered by the Treasury Department. He said:

"That is what I. A. Barnes is here for, as a special employee of the Treasury Department. He has been investigating the appraisement of cattle and their valuation from Mexico. I don't know anything else. Gaither thinks that he has got my scalp and he has told several persons so."

The following morning both Garrett and Gaither paid five-dollar fines for disturbing the peace. Now at last, Secretary Shaw had some solid evidence against Garrett. In order to humiliate Pat to the utmost, Shaw appointed a long-time Garrett enemy, I. A. Barnes, as a "special investigator" who would, supposedly, give an "impartial" report on the brawl. Then—to stick the knife in deeper—Shaw had his assistant send Garrett this scathing rebuke:

TREASURY DEPARTMENT

OFFICE OF THE SECRETARY

Washington,
May 14, 1903

Collector of Customs,
El Paso, Texas.

Sir:

The Department is reliably informed that on the 8th instant you engaged in a disgraceful street brawl with Mr. George M. Gaither, you having first profanely accosted that person, and that both were arrested and fined for such breach of the peace. ﹀

You are directed to submit a prompt and full report upon this subject, and you are advised that such conduct upon the part of a person holding the office of Collector of Customs is regarded as indefensible and deserves censure in the strongest terms.

Respectfully,

R. ACHON

Assistant Secretary.

Pat Garrett was not to be intimidated. On May 21, 1903, he replied to his superior:

While there are extenuating circumstances connected with this unfortunate affair, your letter would indicate that . . . I was entirely in the wrong, no defense could be made for my actions, and that I might expect no consideration. Consequently, I do not deem any report I might make would be construed as justifiable for my conduct.[1]

In the meantime, Garrett brought out his big guns by having his influential friends write endorsements to Secretary Shaw. Foremost among the correspondents was an old Rough Rider buddy of Teddy Roosevelt's:

WILLIAM H. H. LLEWELLYN

Attorney at Law

District Attorney for
Dona Ana, Otero, Luna and Lincoln Counties.

Third Judicial District, New Mexico.

Las Cruces, New Mexico
May 18, 1903.

Hon. Leslie M. Shaw
Secretary Treasury,
Washington, D. C.

My Dear Mr. Secretary,

Living as I do in the El Paso, Texas Collectors district and forty-three miles above the City of El Paso, Texas and knowing Hon. Patrick F. Garrett the Collector of the Port at El Paso, Texas I take the liberty of writing you with reference to him.

Will say that I have known Mr. Garrett for twenty-three years, and also know his history from his boyhood days and I can certify that no more honest, high minded and honorable gentleman ever filled a government position.

During the President's recent trip through New Mexico he very kindly invited me to meet him in Colorado, which I did, and slept in his car one night and was with him at the reception at Santa Fe and Albuquerque.

Mr. Garrett was invited by the President to meet him in Santa Fe and he came down on the train with us as far as Albuquerque and then returned to El Paso.

Mr. Garrett was the President's personal selection for the position which he fills and has the President's confidence and I know the man so well that before he would betray that confidence by doing a dishonorable thing that he would sacrifice his life.

There is a little clique in El Paso who are continually "nagging" at the collector just as they have always done with former collectors, but I know that he has the confidence of the best people of the southwest and I am sure that he will have your entire confidence when you come to know him.

I may be presuming on my short acquaintance with you in writing you this letter, having only had the pleasure of meeting you a few times, but you will remember that when I first met you I presented you a letter from my brother Charles E. Llewellyn who is your devoted friend and admirer as I beg to subscribe myself,

Very respectfully,

W. H. H. LLEWELLYN[2]

NOTES

1. Cited in Leon Metz's, *Pat Garrett: The Story of a Western Lawman*, page 249.

2. William Henry Harrison Llewellyn was born in Monroe, Wisconsin, on September 9, 1853. From 1876 until 1878 he served as Chief Deputy Marshal for the Omaha, Nebraska, district. He married Ida May Little in 1877. They were the parents of eight children.

After being appointed a special agent for the Department of Justice in May, 1879, Llewellyn battled the Doc Middleton gang and formed a close relationship with a future White House Gunfighter named Seth Bullock. Llewellyn and Boone May captured Lew Grimes, who they claimed was killed while trying to excape. The only thing about the incident that seems to be certain is that a shotgun blast from Llewellyn ended Lew Grimes' outlaw career forever. Llewellyn was charged with murder but was acquitted.

In 1880, Llewellyn was appointed Indian Agent on the Mescalero Apache Reservation in New Mexico, and it was about this time that he first made the acquaintance of Pat Garrett. After entering New Mexican politics, Llewellyn became one of the leading lights of the so-called "Santa Fe Ring." Llewellyn served as a member of the Territorial Legislature and was appointed Speaker of the House of that body in 1896.

On February 2, 1896, following the disappearance of Colonel Albert Jennings Fountain and his son, Llewellyn headed up a posse in search of the Fountains and their murderers. The trail led to Oliver Lee's ranch house—but just as Llewellyn's posse approached the ranch, Lee's cowboys drove a herd of cattle between the posse and the ranch, completely obliterating the incriminating trail. Llewellyn's discouraged posse had no choice but to return home.

When the Spanish-American War broke out, Llewellyn and his son joined the Rough Riders. The senior Llewellyn became Captain of Troop G, while his son, Morgan Llewellyn, became a member of Troop A, which was commanded by the flamboyant William Owen "Buckey" O'Neill. Both Llewellyns served with distinction at Las Guasimas, Santiago, and San Juan Hill.

W. H. H. Llewellyn became one of Theodore Roosevelt's favorite officers, and his services were noted by Roosevelt in the book he wrote about his beloved regiment. Said T. R. in his 1899 book:

"Captain Llewellyn was a large, heavy man, who had a grown-up son in the ranks. On the march he had frequently carried the load of some man who weakened . . ." (Theodore Roosevelt, *The Rough Riders*, Charles Scribner's Sons, 1899, page 151) Roosevelt also noted that Llewellyn was "a good citizen, a political leader, and one of the most noted peace-officers of the country; he had been shot four times in pitched fights with red marauders and white outlaws." (Ibid., page 17)

During the brief war, Roosevelt and Llewellyn were frequent companions, and T. R. later recalled that: "A good part of the time I was by Captain Llewellyn, and was greatly pleased to see the way in which he kept his men up to their work. He never pitied or coddled his troopers, but he always looked after them. He helped them whenever he could, and took rather more than his full share of hardship and danger, so that they naturally followed him with entire devotion." (Ibid., page 78)

Following the war, Llewellyn and Pat Garrett organized something called the Alabama Gold and Copper Company, whose "assets" were listed at $200,000—most of this money existing only in the fertile imaginations of Llewellyn and Garrett. The enterprise folded in 1901.

When Theodore Roosevelt became President in 1901, he appointed Llewellyn as Assistant Attorney General, a position he held until 1909.

During the last years, Llewellyn was appointed Attorney for the Third Judicial District of New Mexico by his friend Governor George Curry. Following this, Llewellyn returned to the private practice of law. Failing eyesight and poor health caused him to retire in 1920.

Llewellyn died in Las Cruces on June 11, 1927, at the age of seventy-three.

The only known photograph of Pat Garrett that was made in 1881, the year that he killed Billy the Kid. (Courtesy the Earle Collection.)

Chapter 8

GARRETT CRITICIZED

Unfortunately, the effect of Llewellyn's letter was countered by the indefatigable I. A. Barnes who had gleefully been doing his homework. "Special Employee" Barnes opened his attack on Pat Garrett with these three statements from J. H. Biggs, J. C. Peyton and that *cause celebre* himself—George M. Gaither:

El Paso, Texas
May 22, 1903.

Mr. I. A. Barnes
Special Employee
Treasury Department

Sir:

Complying with your request for a statement of facts regarding the recent Garrett-Gaither street fight, I have to say that on the 8th of May, at about 11:00 A. M., I heard a commotion on the pavement in front of the building occupied by the Nations Meat and Supply Company, where I am employed.

I went out onto the pavement and saw two men fighting, one of whom was Mr. Garrett, the Collector of Customs, and the other Mr. George Gaither. I furthermore noticed that one of the participants was bleeding and I tried to separate the fighters by getting between them, but was unable to accomplish this.

Then seeing that some man had his arms around Mr. Gaither's waist endeavoring to pull him away from the affray, I thereupon took hold of Mr. Garrett in the same manner and for the same purpose, and in this way the fight was stopped.

Respectfully,

J. H. BIGGS

El Paso, Texas
May 22, 1903.

Mr. I. A. Barnes,
Special Employee,
Treasury Department,
City.

Sir:

In compliance with your request for a statement as to the conversation which I heard between Mr. P. F. Garrett and Mr. George M. Gaither, on the morning of the 8th instant, just previous to their engaging in a fight, I have to state that on my way up stairs to see Mr. Nations, on business, I stopped to say good morning to Colonel Evans and Mr. Gaither, who were standing at the foot of the stairs conversing.

Presently Mr. Garrett came up and said to Mr. Gaither: "Did you tell Mr. Buchoz that I said that I would give you a permanent position?"

"I told Mr. Buchoz that Colonel Evans told me you would give me a permanent position," was Gaither's reply as near as I can remember the wording.

Mr. Garrett's answer to this was: "You are a damned liar."

Respectfully,

J. C. PEYTON

El Paso, Texas
May 22, 1903.

Mr. I. A. Barnes,
Special Agent,
Treasury Department,
City.

Sir:

In compliance with your request of the 20th instant to submit my version of the recent fight which occured between Mr. P. F. Garrett and myself, I have to say that on the morning of the 8th instant, shortly before 11:00 A. M., I was standing on San Antonio

Street near the Nations Meat and Supply Company building talking to Colonel Evans and Mr. Peyton.

Mr. Garrett came up to me and said: "Did you tell Buchoz that I said the position you had was permanent?"

I said: "No, I did not, but said that you promised, with the assistance of Colonel Evans, if possible, to make it permanent."

Thereupon Mr. Garrett said: "You're a God damned liar."

I immediately struck him and we commenced fighting. We were separated and, in endeavoring to get together again to continue our fighting, Mr. Garrett turned to Colonel Evans and said, "You're a God damned liar."

Respectfully,

GEO. M. GAITHER

Also included in Barnes' package to Secretary Shaw was a letter from Pat Garrett. Since Garrett had already, in effect, told the Secretary of the Treasury himself to go to hell the previous day, he wasn't about to favor the low-ranking "Special Employee," I. A. Barnes, with a statement:

CUSTOMS SERVICE

OFFICE OF THE COLLECTOR

El Paso, Tex.,
May 22, 1903

Mr. I. A. Barnes,
Special Employee,
El Paso, Texas.

Sir:

Referring to your letter of the 21st instant, requesting a statement in writing of the facts in the case of the street fight between George M. Gaither and myself, some time since, I have to reply that in view of the contents of the Department letter of the 14th instant, from which I am given to understand I have no defense or excuse for my conduct, or would such be considered, I cannot see what good results would be obtained by a statement from me.

CUSTOMS SERVICE,
OFFICE OF THE COLLECTOR,

CAK. EL PASO, TEX., April 7, 1903.

The honorable the Secretary of the Treasury,

Washington, D. C.

Sir:

I have the honor to enclose herewith the oath of office of
Mr. George M. Gaither, appointed temporary special inspector on
March 9, 1903, for a period of thirty days at a compensation of
$3.00 per diem.

The opinions of the Special Agent at this port and myself,
have been at variance regarding the values placed on Mexican cattle
imported at this port, and after consultation it was agreed to
appoint some disinterested person for a limited time, to inquire,
and ascertain if possible, the situation of the cattle markets
in Mexico looking toward a closer agreement between the two offices
upon the question involved.

Mr. Gaither was selected by the Special Agent as the proper
person to secure this information, and as his term of office
expires to day, and his services of no further material value for
the purpose for which he was appointed, I respectfully request my
action be approved and authority be granted to pay him.

Respectfully,

Patrick F. Garrett

Collector of Customs.

You are to infer from this letter that I have no moral objection to
making a statement of facts in the case, but having been tried and adjudged upon malicious statements, without an opportunity to present
my case, I have to respectfully decline to accede to your request.

Respectfully,

PATRICK F. GARRETT

Collector of Customs.

Before concluding his investigation, Special Employee
Barnes sent Secretary Shaw this follow-up report containing the
statements of Joseph F. Evans and Maury Kemp:

CUSTOMS SERVICE,
OFFICE OF THE COLLECTOR,

CAK.

EL PASO, TEX. May 22, 1903.

Mr. I. A. Barnes,

Special Employe,

El Paso, Texas.

Sir:

Referring to your letter of the 21st instant, requesting a statement in writing of the facts in the case of the street fight between George M. Gaither and myself, some time since, I have to reply that in view of the contents of Department letter of the 14th instant, from which I am given to understand I have no defense or excuse for my conduct, or would much be considered, I cannot see what good results would be obtained by a statement from me.

You are to infer from this letter that I have no moral objection to making a statement of facts in the case, but having been tried and adjudged upon malicious statements, without an opportunity to present my case, I have to respectfully decline to accede to your request.

Respectfully,

Patrick F. Garrett

Collector of Customs.

OFFICE OF SPECIAL AGENT

TREASURY DEPARTMENT

El Paso, Texas,
May 27, 1903.

To the Honorable
The Secretary of the Treasury
Washington, D. C.

Sir:

Referring to my report of the 22nd instant, concerning the recent street fight which took place in this city, between Mr. P. F. Garrett,

Colonel Theodore Roosevelt,
as commander of
the Rough Riders.

Collector of Customs, and Mr. George M. Gaither, I now have the honor to enclose a statement of facts signed by Mr. Joseph F. Evans, marked "Exhibit H," and also a similar statement signed by Mr. Maury Kemp, marked "Exhibit I."

Both of these gentlemen were out of the city when I made my previous report, and it was impossible to obtain their statements until to-day. Mr. Kemp is the County Attorney for El Paso County.

If desired, I can obtain statements from the officers who made the arrests and from other witnesses to the affair, but have thought it unnecessary to submit additional details of this occurrence, which many of the citizens consider a very disgraceful affair.

Respectfully,

I. A. BARNES

Special Employee.

El Paso, Texas
May 27, 1903

Mr. I. A. Barnes
Special Employee,
El Paso.

Sir:

On the morning of May 8th instant about 10 o'clock I went to the office of Mr. J. H. Nation. On my way I met Mr. Gaither who turned about and walked with me until we reached the stairway to Mr. Nation's office when I told him where I was going and asked to walk upstairs as I would detain him but a minute.

He declined and while we were talking I saw Collector Garrett approaching, walking rapidly, and when he reached us he accosted Gaither by asking him if he had said that he, Garrett, had promised to appoint him to office for 60 or so days, to which Gaither replied that he said as much, when Garrett using vile language and in a wrath called him a God d----d liar and Gaither struck him.

As the relations between the Collector and myself, both personal and official, up to that time had been of a cordial character, I caught him by the arm and said, "for God sake don't engage in a street fight!" But they did fight until separated by two strong policemen.

Ugly words and oaths were used by Collector Garrett and some of them were applied to me, since which time I have had no conversation with the Collector except upon official business.

Very respectfully,

JOSEPH F. EVANS

Special Agent,
Treasy. Dept.

El Paso, Texas
May 27th, 1903.

Mr. I. A. Barnes,
Treasury Department,
El Paso, Texas.

Dear Sir:

In compliance with your request of this day to give a statement as to the difficulty that occurred between Mr. Pat Garrett, the Collector of Customs at this port, and Mr. George Gaither of this place, I beg to say:

On the morning of the 8th of May, 1903, I was on my way to my office passing down San Antonio Street, walking on the left hand side of the street, going toward El Paso Street.

About the time that I arrived in front of the J. H. Nations Meat & Supply Co., shop, I saw two men standing immediately in front of the entrance to the stairway of the Turner Building; both men seemed very angry and were talking quite loud, though I could not understand what was being said.

A second later both men began to strike at each other, and a lively fight ensued. At that time I did not know who either of the parties were, but ran quickly up to where they were and found one to be Mr. Garrett and the other to be Mr. Gaither.

I took hold of Mr. Gaither as best I could and pulled him away from Mr. Garrett, while the Chief of Police, Mr. Peyton Edwards, took hold of Mr. Garrett and kept him from striking Mr. Gaither. As soon as this was done the two men walked quickly away in opposite directions.

Both men were very angry and excited, and both equally eager to fight. As to which of the two men struck the first blow I cannot say, as I did not recognize either of them when the trouble first arose.

After the Chief of the Police and I succeeded in getting the two men separated, Mr. Gaither accused Mr. Garrett of having told him, Gaither a lie . . . Garrett, in response to having been called a liar by Mr. Gaither, replied that Mr. Gaither was a son-of-a-bitch, or more accurately, I believe he said "a damn son-of-a bitch," and that the Colonel was "too."

Mr. Garrett almost immediately after having made this remark turned and went down the street, Mr. Gaither doing like wise, except going in the opposite direction, up the street. This I believe is all that I saw and heard.

Very truly yours,

MAURY KEMP

With Barnes' report, the investigation into the Gaither episode was concluded; but it was obvious that Secretary Shaw was still out to get Garrett's scalp. At one point Shaw wrote: "Reports from many sources indicate that you are not doing your full duty in fixing the correct market price of cattle admitted to the United States."[1]

The Secretary then urged Garrett to give "personal attention to and require indication on every entry of the specific class of cattle imported sufficient to enable our special representatives[2] to trace actual conditions in each case."[3]

Garrett replied angrily on June 20, 1903, that his handling of the cattle situation was "connected with many details which are difficult to explain when investigation is conducted with a view in mind to make the most of trivial discrepancies that arise in the transactions of business. Pat also blamed his latest difficulty on the "adverse and exaggerated reports" made to Secretary Shaw by Special Agent Joseph F. Evans. Pat claimed that Evans' statements were based upon "stories poured into the ear of ready listeners for the purpose of causing conflict."[4]

NOTES

1. Cited in Metz, *Patrick Garrett: The Story of a Western Lawman*, page 249.
2. These "special representatives" were none other than Pat Garrett's arch-foes, Joseph F. Evans and I. A. Barnes.
3. Metz, *Pat Garrett*, page 249.
4. Ibid., page 250.

Emerson Hough (1857-1923) was a noted author of his day and a close friend of Pat Garrett and Theodore Roosevelt. (Courtesy of Leon Metz.)

Chapter 9

EMERSON HOUGH

It was in the midst of all this personal misery that Pat Garrett made the acquaintance of the noted writer, Emerson Hough,[1] who happened to be a very close friend of Theodore Roosevelt. Garrett had contacted Hough with the proposal that they co-author an updated version of Garrett's 1882 book, *The Authentic Life of Billy the Kid.* By 1904 there were few copies to be found. The sole copy of the 1882 edition, possessed by Pat Garrett, had fallen apart years earlier and the remaining pages were tied together by string.

Garrett mailed Hough the decaying copy of his 1882 book to rewrite. Hough, being more practical than romantic, first decided to test the waters by writing Garrett's story as a magazine article. Once this was done, he returned the copy of Garrett's battered book, along with his article manuscript, to Pat with this letter:

June 30, 1904

Hon. Pat F. Garrett,
Collector of Customs,
El Paso, Texas.

Dear Pat:

I am sending you herewith a duplicate Ms. of my Lincoln County War story for McClure's magazine. I wrote out my notes and had about three times the number of pages shown here.

I am afraid the story is too long, even now, for magazine purposes, but this will show you my scheme of the material and enable you to tell how yourself and friends have been handled.

I did not want to hurt any one's feelings, and of course wanted to tell nothing but the truth. You had better mark on this copy any corrections you think needful and return it to me, and in case McClures want the story, all these corrections will go into type as you make them.

If they do not want it—and of course we can never tell about these things—then it will find print somewhere else in due time, I am quite sure.

Life seems to be awfully short up here in Chicago, and it is hard for me to get away, but some time I am coming down into that country and ride all over it with you. We will be able to write enough to pay expenses any how, I am confident.

I am sending you herewith also the fragments of your book, you will see kept carefully and even with the same red string around it. I was never able to get another copy of the book. We ought to get a complete copy of this somewhere.

When we are both a little less busy, we might practically re-write that and get together a volume which would be more lasting and which, as you say, would be a record for your children. I am keeping that in mind all the time, and will preserve all of this material which I have not used in the story.

I have been half hoping that you would come up here this summer and drop in for a visit. Mrs. Hough and I will be mighty glad to see you and will take care of you here.

Mrs. Hough is pretty well—a little scared yet over her life in Lincoln. We still have hopes of catching Mrs. Garrett sometime when she is not looking. Let me hear from you, and believe me always

Your friend,

EMERSON HOUGH

Another six months passed before Pat Garrett got this good news in the form of a letter from his friend Emerson Hough:

January 3, 1905.

Pat F. Garrett, Esq.,
Collector of Customs,
El Paso, Texas.

Dear Mr. Garrett:

I had about concluded to run my Lincoln County War stuff in

Field and Stream, when I met Mr. Lorimer, Editor of the *Saturday Evening Post* of Philadelphia, a very wealthy paper.

I told Mr. Lorimer of your talk to me in which you said you some time wanted to take a ride over all the old scenes in New Mexico with a view to the story of your earlier life in that country.

Mr. Lorimer said he would like to print that in the *Post.* I told him I could not afford to take the time and money for such a trip, unless he would definitely agree to pay for the stuff. This he said he would do.

I then told him I was thinking of running my Lincoln County stuff in *Field and Stream,* but he said this would kill our story for the *Post,* although he would have no objection to my running it in *Field and Stream* after the *Post* had had it's first shot at the material.

We set no time for my coming down to the Territory. I could not get away before spring. Do you think you can ever take the time to make that little ride as we talked it over? It seems to me we will get together a bunch of material which would surely do for a book at some time.

I do not know of any one who could do that better than myself, as I already know that country. Think this over and write me some time whether you think you would like to ride with me over the old country once more.

I really feel ashamed of the long delay in getting this New Mexican stuff into print, but you must understand that the ways of publishers are very slow and frequently very tricky.

McClure's promised to use this stuff, but threw me down at the last moment, and incidentally cost me about $600 which I spent in gathering material. It will, however, come into play some time, and I hope you will not then regret having spent a few hours with me.

I am very busy with my novels, which pay me very well, but some time I will get time to write out a book on famous fights and feuds, in which the old country and yourself will have full prominence; or, if I did not do that, I could if you preferred it, re-work the old Billy the Kid material into a book devoted to yourself.

The only trouble is to get the time and to get a publisher who would make it worth while for both of us. Don't think I am any quitter on this, for I will surely do it some time.

Mrs. Hough adds her regards, and we hope to see you again some time this year.

Yours sincerely,

EMERSON HOUGH

Tom Powers with two Appaloosa horses in about 1908 in front of the El Paso County Courthouse. (Courtesy of the Powers Collection, U.T. El Paso Archives.)

It was almost three months before Emerson Hough again contacted Pat Garrett regarding the possibility of a western junket:

March 29, 1905

Hon. Pat F. Garrett
Collector of Customs,
El Paso, Texas.

Dear Pat Garrett:

Mr. Lorimer, editor of the *Saturday Evening Post*, was here last week, and he gave me orders for several Western stories. He thinks I can get all the data for this in New Mexico, which is not the case, but as he wishes me to take the Western trip, I am going to make that ride with you.

We could get together material to piece the old "Billy the Kid" book, if we can do nothing better, and sometime we will get a publisher. I think The Outing publishing company of New York would like to look at some such book.

The trouble about doing it is that it would not sell so well as a novel, and I have been obliged to do the things which paid best. I think I could squeeze in time to fix out this book, however, and will talk it over when I see you.

I shall be here until after the first of May, but would like to join you sometime in the month of May, as near as I can tell now. It will be pretty hot by that time, but this is the best I can do.

I will keep in touch with you, and we will have a good time when we get started, and I hope there will some good come of it afterward. I wish you were up here this spring.

My health has not been very good, and I look forward to this trip to help me. It will be a great delight to see the old country again.

Always yours sincerely,

EMERSON HOUGH

The plans for a get-together between Garrett and Hough had to be postponed when the latter came down with typhoid fever. In the meantime, something happened that really boosted Pat's sagging spirits; President Roosevelt was planning to attend a Rough Riders' reunion in San Antonio during April, 1905, and invited Pat to attend as his special guest. This was a genuine sign of Presidential favor since Pat had not been a member of the noted regiment.

Pat asked if he could bring a friend and—of all people— chose Tom Powers who was the proprietor of the Coney Island Saloon, which was then considered to be one of El Paso's most notorious dives. At the reunion, Garrett introduced Powers to the President as a "cattleman," rather than as the gambler and saloon keeper that Powers really was.

The real trouble began when photographers snapped two photos of the President in the company of Garrett and Powers. One of these photos showed a dapper Pat Garrett and Tom Powers seated directly across from the President at the banquet table. After the President returned to Washington, Garrett's enemies lost no time in informing Roosevelt of Powers' actual

background, and that Roosevelt hadn't brought any credit upon
his administration by being photographed with a notorious
character such as Tom Powers.

In the meantime, Emerson Hough was making a slow recovery from his illness and had to postpone his meeting with Pat
Garrett once more:

May 2, 1905

Hon. Pat F. Garrett
Collector of Customs,
El Paso, Texas.

Dear Mr. Garrett:

This is the third week I have been in bed with typhoid fever and
they cannot tell just yet when I will be up. As soon as I can I will let
you know and start for the southwest.

Two publishing firms want to look at this western material of
ours. One is here in Chicago, and although the material is not in shape
I may get some sort of notion from them as to what they can do.

I will try to have something to tell you by the time I meet you.
This sickness has knocked out a great many of my plans.

Mrs. Hough joins me in regards.

Sincerely yours,

EMERSON HOUGH

Two months after writing this letter, Hough still didn't feel
up to the trip and decided to revise his schedule once more:

July 19, 1905.

Hon. Pat F. Garrett,
Collector of Customs,
El Paso, Texas.

Dear Mr. Garrett:

I will put off the New Mexico trip as late as the editor of *The
Saturday Evening Post* will permit, and I will advise you well in ad-

*A photograph that has long
been claimed to be Billy
the Kid. (Courtesy Rose
Collection, University
of Oklahoma.)*

vance of the date when I shall start for the Southwest, so that you may have ample time to get things arranged.

We do not want to stay out too long, and of course we do not want to make hard work of it. I think we would both enjoy a little expedition of that kind.

It seems hard to handle this material in book form, but I have placed the matter before a publisher using the services of a literary agent who lives in New York. I do not think there is any doubt that we will be able to get a publisher sometime.

I have been reluctant to lay aside other work and do the writing on this book until I had some kind of an understanding made with the publisher. These things come slow, but we will surely get there, and I think you will not regret any expenditure of time you may have made.

I am sorry you have been sick. There seems to be no time or place in these days for sickness. Personally, I am slowly recovering from my experience, and hope to be able to ride all right when I see you in the fall.

Mrs. Hough joins me in best regards.

Yours sincerely,

EMERSON HOUGH

CUSTOMS SERVICE

OFFICE OF THE COLLECTOR

El Paso, Tex.,
July 25, 1905.

Mr. Emerson Hough,
First National Bank Building,
Chicago, Ill.

Dear Mr. Hough:

Yours of July 19th to hand. I note what you say about our prospective trip and will try and be ready when you reach here.

In my opinion the best point from which to be outfitted to start overland would be at Tularosa, New Mexico. We should not undertake this trip later than October, for after the first of November we would more than likely strike a Norther and get into a cold streak of weather. I will be ready and look for you by the first of October at any rate.

Remember me very kindly to Mrs. Hough, and believe me,

Most sincerely yours,

PATRICK F. GARRETT

NOTES

1. Emerson Hough (pronounced Huff) was born on June 28, 1857, in Newton, Iowa. Hough received his law degree from the University of Iowa and was admitted to the bar. The practice of law was not to his liking, and he began selling stories to the popular magazines of his day. For awhile, he was employed by newspapers in Des Moines, Iowa, and Sandusky, Ohio. Later, he moved to Chicago where he managed the branch office of *Field and Stream*.

Hough loved to wander and didn't stay in one place long; he had explored Yellowstone Park on skis during the winter of 1895. An act of Congress protecting the park's buffalo herd was a direct result of this trip.

After marrying Charlotte A. Cheseborough on October 28, 1897, Hough made his headquarters—more or less—in Chicago. During that same year, his first book, *The Story of the Cowboy*, was published, but it wasn't until 1902 with the publication of *The Mississippi Bubble*, that Hough was able to live wholly by his writing.

Hough had formed a friendship with Theodore Roosevelt in the 1890s and maintained a regular correspondence with him. He first made the acquaintance of Pat Garrett about 1903 and managed to persuade the old gunfighter to take time off from his stormy career as Collector of Customs to help him do research in Lincoln County, New Mexico.

One day as Hough and Garrett were riding near Roswell, New Mexico, a startled deer dashed across their path. Garrett grabbed his rifle, and it misfired. "The last time that gun did that," Garrett explained sadly, "I had Oliver Lee (one of the Fountain murder suspects) in my sights!"

In collaborating with Garrett, Hough's original intention had been to update Garrett's 1882 book, *The Authentic Life of Billy the Kid*, but Hough had to shelve the idea after discussing it with his publisher, who wanted a book containing a series of chapters dealing with several western gunfighters. Thus, Billy the Kid simply became one of the many subjects in a 1906 book entitled, *The Story of the Outlaw*.

Pat Garrett read and made improvements in the Lincoln County portion of the manuscript but saw all his efforts wasted when the publishers edited the book to make it more romantic and entertaining than truthful.

Hough went on to write another twenty-five novels with *The Covered Wagon* being the best known today. Although he wasn't, in any sense of the term, a great writer, Hough thought he was. In time, his obsession with the western types he wrote about totally absorbed him.

Perhaps his friend, Charles C. Baldwin, summed it up best when he wrote that Hough "ran away from life; from his fellows; he hid in the forests; he played at being back in the days of the great explorers."

The nomadic Emerson Hough died at age sixty-five on August 30, 1923.

Refugio Espalin, twin brother of Jose Espalin, Garrett's deputy in Las Cruces. (Courtesy of Anita Espalin.)

Chapter 10

A VISIT TO LINCOLN COUNTY

Emerson Hough recovered his health in time to get together with Pat Garrett during October, 1905, when Garrett finally gave the author a personal guided tour of Lincoln County, New Mexico. The initial result of their trip was an article for the *Saturday Evening Post.* That article was reprinted in the *El Paso Herald* of Saturday, December 9, 1905:

PAT GARRETT AND THE "WILD WEST"

Emerson Hough Tells of the Stirring Days in New Mexico
When "Billy the Kid" and Other Outlaws Were at Large,
When Blood Ran Over Every Inch of Lincoln County
and Garrett was Helping to Advance Civilization's
Onward March With the Aid of Revolver and Cartridge.

Recent Visit to the Old Battleground.

Emerson Hough, the well-known author of western stories, has a very interesting article in this week's *Saturday Evening Post* on the western bad man, in which he devotes considerable space to the days when Pat Garrett was sheriff of Lincoln County, including an account of the killing of "Billie (sic) the Kid" by Garrett while in office.

Hough and Mr. Garrett recently made a trip through the section of country over which Garrett presided as sheriff and telling of this trip, Hough says:

As I lived in that country myself at the time of Pat Garrett's tenure as sheriff in Lincoln County, we two had planned a land voyage of some 500 or 600 miles, with the purpose of visiting certain old scenes together. We were now driving across the wind-swept plateau near old Fort Sumner. When near the edge of the Pecos Valley he reined up and pointed to the southward.

"Down there, eight or ten miles," said he, "there used to be a little saloon, and I took a man there once. He came in from somewhere east, and was wanted for murder. The reward offered for him was $1200.

As he was a stranger, none of us knew him, but the sheriff's description sent in said he had a freckled face, small hands, and a red spot in his eye. I heard that there was a new saloon keeper in there, and thought he might be the man, so I took a deputy and went down one day to see.

The Man With the Red Eye.

"I told my deputy not to shoot until he saw me go after my gun. I didn't want to hold the man up unless he was the right one; and I wanted to be sure about that identification mark in the eye.

"Now when a bartender is waiting on you he will never look you in the face until just as you raise your glass to drink. I told my deputy that we would order a couple of drinks and so get a chance to look this fellow in the eye. I did look him in the eye—and there was the red spot!

"I dropped my glass and jerked my gun and covered him, but he just wouldn't put up his hands for a while. I didn't want to kill him, but I thought I surely would have to. He kept both of his hands resting on the bar and I knew he had a gun within three feet of him somewhere. At last he slowly gave in.

"I treated him well, as I always did a prisoner. We put the irons on him and started for Las Vegas with him in a wagon. The next morning out he confessed everything to me. We turned him over, and later he was tried and hung. I don't remember his name. I always considered him to be a bad man. So far as the outcome was concerned, he might about as well have gone after his gun.

Nervy Man.

"One of the nerviest men I ever ran against," the ex-sheriff went on reflectively, "I met when I was sheriff of Dona Ana County. I was in Las Cruces, when there came in a sheriff from over in the Indian Nations, looking for a fugitive who had broken out of the penitentiary after killing a guard and another man or so.

"This sheriff told me that the criminal in question was the most desperate man he had ever known, and that no matter how we came on him he would put up a fight, and we would have to kill him before we could take him.

We located our man, who was cooking on a ranch six or eight miles out of town. I told the sheriff to stay in town, as our man would know him and would not know us. I had a Mexican deputy along with me.

Charles Bowdre, a member
of the Kid's gang was
killed by Garrett's posse
in December of 1880
at Stinking Springs.

"I put out my deputy on one side of the house and went in. I found my man just washing his hands on a towel after washing up his dishes. I threw down on him and he answered by knocking me down with his fist and jumping through the window like a squirrel.

"I caught at him and tore the shirt off his back, but did not stop him. Then I ran out the door and caught him on the porch. I did not want to kill him, so I struck him over the head with the handcuffs I had ready for him. He dropped, but came up like a flash and struck me so hard with his fist that I was good and jarred.

Fought Desperately.

"We fought hammer and tongs for a while, but at length he broke away, sprang through the door, and ran down the hall. He was going to his room after his gun. Just then my Mexican came in, and, having no sentiment about it, just whaled away and shot him in the back, killing him on the spot.

"The doctors said, when they examined the man's body, that he was the most perfect physical specimen they had ever seen. I have forgotten this man's name too, but I can testify he was a fighter.[1]

"The sheriff offered me the reward, but I would not take any of it. I told him I would be looking for some one over in his country some day and was sure he would do as much for me."

A Bad Bunch.

It was at old Fort Sumner, as many in the southwest may remember, that, in his first term of office as sheriff, Pat Garrett was
called on to capture the notorious young desperado, Billy the Kid,
then not over 20 years of age, but charged with nearly a dozen murders—most say he had killed 21 men; Garrett says nine.

With the Kid at their chosen headquarters about nine miles east
of Fort Sumner were Tom Pickett, one of Lincoln County's war
fighters; Tom O'Folliard, another reckless character charged with
murder; Dave Rudabaugh, who had killed his jailer at Las Vegas, and
Charley Bowdre, formerly a small rancher on the Bonito, but of late
turned killer.

Garrett concealed his deputies in houses at Fort Sumner and put
out scouts. One day he and some of his men were riding eastward of
the town when they jumped Tom O'Folliard, who was mounted on a
horse that proved too good for them in a chase of several miles.

Garrett at last was left alone following O'Folliard. The latter
later admitted that he fired 20 times at Garrett with his Winchester,
but it was hard to do good shooting from the saddle at two or three
hundred yards' range, so neither man was hit.

O'Folliard did not learn his lesson. A few nights later, in company
with Tom Pickett, he rode boldly into town. Warned of his approach,
Garrett, with another man, was waiting, hid in the shadow of a building. As O'Folliard rode up he was ordered to throw up his hands, but
went after his gun instead, and on the instant was shot through the
body.

Lost Nerve When Shot.

"You never heard a man scream the way he did," said Garrett.
"He dropped his gun when he was hit, but we did not know that, and
as we ran up to catch his horse we ordered him to throw up his hands.
He said he couldn't, that he was killed. We helped him down then, and
took him in the house. He died about 5 minutes later. He said it was
all his own fault and that he didn't blame anybody.[2]

"I'd have killed Tom Pickett right there too," concluded Garrett,
"but one of my men shot right past my face and blinded me for a
moment, so Pickett got away."

Kid to Help Officers.

The remainder of the Kid's gang moved out a little farther into a
stone house, ten miles from Fort Sumner, but this new refuge proved

A photograph that many claim to be Billy the Kid. (Courtesy of the Rose Collection, University of Oklahoma.)

to be a veritable trap for them. Garrett and his men surrounded the house just before dawn. It was Charley Bowdre who first came out in the morning, and as he stepped in the doorway his career as a bad man ended, three bullets passing through his body.[3]

The rest of the gang later surrendered and were taken to Santa Fe. Here the officers had their most dangerous experience, for a mob was formed which stopped the railroad train in the depot yards, threatening to kill both prisoners and officers. As Garrett had accepted the surrender of the prisoners on the condition that they should all be taken safely to Santa Fe, he felt both his life and honor at stake.

"Give me a six-shooter, Pat," said Billy the Kid, "and if they come in the car I'll help you and I won't hurt you, and if they don't kill me I'll go back to my seat when it's over. You and I can whip the whole of them."

This compact between the bad man and his captor was actually made, but at the last moment the leaders of the mob weakened and the train pulled out.[4]

The End of William

Later Billy the Kid was tried at Mesilla, and condemned to be executed at Lincoln. A few days before the day set for his execution he killed the two deputies, Orrendorf (sic) and Bell, who were guarding him, and broke back to his old stamping grounds around Fort Sumner.[5]

"I knew now that I would have to kill the Kid," said Garrett speaking reminiscently of the old bloody scenes, "I followed him up to Sumner, as you know, with two deputies, John Poe and Tip McKinney, and I killed him alone in a room up there in the old Maxwell house."[6]

He spoke of events now long gone by. It had been only with difficulty that we located the site of the building where the Kid's gang had been taken prisoners, the structure itself having been torn down and removed by an adjacent sheep rancher.

As to old Fort Sumner, once a famous military post, it offered nothing better than a scene of desolation, there being no longer a single human inhabitant there. The old avenue of cottonwoods, once four miles long, is now ragged and unwatered, and the great parade ground has gone back to sand and sage brush.

We were obliged to search for some time before we could find the site of the Maxwell house, in which was enacted the last tragedy of a once famous bad man. Garrett finally located the spot, now only a rough quadrangle of crumbled earthern walls.

Where Billy Bit the Dust.

"This is the place." said he, pointing at one corner of the grass-grown oblong. "Pete Maxwell's bed was right in this corner of the room, and I was sitting in the dark and talking to Pete, who was in bed. The Kid passed John Poe and Tip McKinney, my deputies, right over there on what then was the gallery, and came through the door right here.

"He could not tell who I was. 'Pete,' he whispered, 'who is it?'

"He had his pistol, a double-action 41. in his hand, and he spoke, still not recognizing me. That was about all there was to it.

"I supposed he would shoot me, and I leaned over to the left so that he would hit me in the right side and not kill me so dead but what I could kill him too. I was just a shade too quick for him. His

Tom O'Folliard, the Kid's closest friend and constant companion.

pistol went off as he fell, but I don't suppose he ever knew who killed him or how he was killed."

Graves of Three Bad Ones.

Twenty-five years of time had done their work in all that country, as we learned when we entered the little barbed-wire inclosure of the cemetery where the Kid and his fellows were buried. There are no headstones in this cemetery, and no sacristan holds its records. Again Garrett had to search in the salt grass and greasewood.

"Here is the place," said he at length. "We buried them all in a row. The first grave is the Kid's and next to him is Bowdre, and then O'Folliard. There's nothing left to mark them."

So passes the glory of this world. Even the headboard which once stood at the Kid's grave—and which was once riddled with bullets by cowards who would not have dared to shoot that close to him had he been alive—was gone. It is not likely that the graves will be visited again by anyone who knows their locality.

Garrett looked at them in silence for a time, and turning, went to the buckboard for a drink at the canteen. "Well," said he quietly, "here's to the boys, anyway. If there is any other life, I hope they'll make better use of it than they did the one I put them out of."

Brave Men's Sons.

As between Pat Garrett and Billy the Kid, for instance, a case of a good man and a bad man, neither was afraid of the other. Each had qualities the other respected. We talked over some of these things philosophically.

"I believe a man who wants to do what is right is braver than the one who does not," said Garrett. "Also, I believe that to be clean game a man has got to be well born. Now, I couldn't imagine that any one of my boys would ever be a coward."

NOTES

1. The incident Garrett described, fairly accurately, was the killing of Norman Newman at the San Augustine Ranch on October 7, 1899. Newman was wanted for murder in Greer County, Oklahoma. Sheriff George Blalock of Greer County, journeyed to New Mexico to enlist Garrett's assistance in capturing the fugitive. The "Mexican deputy" Garrett credits with firing the fatal shot was named Jose Espalin.

2. The killing of Tom O'Folliard happened on December 19, 1880. Garrett and his deputy, Lon Chambers, both fired at O'Folliard, although Garrett is usually credited with the fatal shot. O'Folliard lingered in great agony for some forty-five minutes (rather than the "five minutes" stated in this account) before dying.

3. The killing of Charlie Bowdre on December 22, 1880, happened at a place that was actually called "Sinking Springs"—but that is erroneously referred to as "Stinking Springs" in nearly all accounts of the event.

4. The incident described actually took place in Las Vegas—not Santa Fe—New Mexico, on December 27, 1880. Billy the Kid remained nonplused during the threat upon his life, and told a reporter "if I only had my Winchester I'd lick the whole crowd."

5. Billy the Kid was brought to Lincoln on April 21, 1881, and lodged in an upstairs room of the Lincoln County courthouse. Sheriff Pat Garrett had assigned his deputies, James W. Bell and Robert Ameridth Olinger, with the task of guarding the Kid. For a week everything went fine. Then, on April 28, 1881, while Sheriff Garrett was out of town, the Kid managed to kill both his guards and escape.

6. See Chapter 3, Note 6.

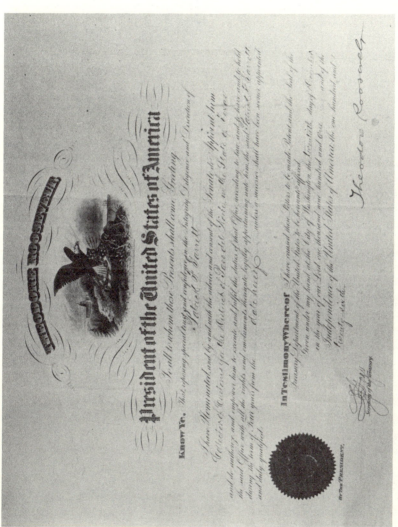

Pat F. Garrett's commission as Collector of Customs. (Courtesy of Richard Marohn)

Teddy Roosevelt's favorite photograph of himself that was taken in 1912. (Jack DeMattos Collection.)

Chapter 11

DISMISSAL FROM OFFICE

The lengthy article by Emerson Hough proved to be the last good press notice that Pat Garrett received in his lifetime. The day after it appeared, Sunday, December 10, 1905, a man named A. L. Sharpe met with President Roosevelt; the hot rumor was that Sharpe had been chosen to replace Pat Garrett as El Paso's Collector of Customs.

In a last ditch effort to save his job, Garrett went to Washington to see the President. Incredibly—and over the objections of his friends—Pat took Tom Powers along with him! Pat met with the President on December 11 and received a frigid reception. Roosevelt made it clear that Powers was not welcome to the Executive Mansion and was to be excluded from the interview; by the time Garrett left he realized that he would no longer be welcomed at the White House either.[1]

The El Paso *Herald* of December 12, 1905, gave front page coverage to Pat's troubles:

GARRETT AND TOM POWERS ARE NOW IN WASHINGTON

Sharpe and Garrett Have Both Seen the President
Regarding Customs Collectorship Here.

WASHINGTON, Dec. 12.—Concerned apparently by the presence of J. A. Smith and A. L. Sharpe in Washington for the purpose of trying to obtain for the latter the position of Collector of Customs at El Paso, Pat Garrett, the present collector, has come on from Texas, accompanied by his friend, Tom Powers, the saloon man and gambling house proprietor, also of El Paso, who took lunch with the President on the occasion of the Rough Riders' reunion at San Antonio last spring, as Garrett's guest.

Messrs. Sharpe and Smith had a conference with the President Sunday and Collector Garrett had an engagement at 11 o'clock yesterday morning. The outcome is in doubt, but there are numerous straws which indicate which way the wind is blowing and certain facts in connection with the case promise some developments.

So far National Committeeman Lyon has taken no part in the contest, as up to this time the President has persisted in looking on the appointment as belonging to New Mexico instead of Texas.

The following day the press made the rumors official and this account of Garrett's dismissal was given in the El Paso *Herald* of December 13, 1905:

PRESIDENT HAS DECLINED TO REAPPOINT PAT GARRETT

Declares That He Will No Longer Consider the Appointment
a Personal One, and Mr. Shaw at Once Recommends
A. L. Sharpe, Who Is Endorsed
By State Chairman Lyon.

Custom House Employees Send Endorsements for Garrett.

WASHINGTON, Dec. 13.—It is said that the President has emphatically declined to reappoint Pat Garrett Collector of Customs at El Paso.

The President called for all papers in the case and after examining them, notified Secretary Shaw that the position was no longer to be regarded as a personal appointment.

Shaw immediately recommended A. L. Sharpe and, as Sharpe has State Chairman Lyon's endorsement, it is probable he will secure the appointment.

The announcement may not be made for a fortnight yet.

Houston Hears the News.

HOUSTON, TEX., Dec. 13.—A special from Washington to the *Chronicle* says Pat Garrett will not be reappointed collector of the port of El Paso and if a Texas is recognized it will be A. L. Sharpe whose chances are considered excellent.

The first definite news from the El Paso Customs Collectorship race to reach El Paso came yesterday. The first information was a telegram from Pat Garrett, the present collector, who is seeking reappointment, stating that the President had decided to appoint a Texan to the place and that he would not succeed himself.

Last night a telegram came to *The Herald* stating that the President had declined to appoint Mr. Garrett and that probably he would name A. L. Sharpe, the other applicant for the place, and the candidate of the regular Republican organization, who is there with J. A. Smith seeking the job.

The dispatch stated, as printed above, that the President declares he no longer considers the appointment a personal one and that Secretary Shaw consequently has recommended Mr. Sharpe. This news was confirmed further in a telegram this morning to the *Herald* from Houston, repeating a Washington dispatch to the *Chronicle*.

Subordinates At Work.

Collector Garrett's telegram was addressed to his chief deputy, Numa Buchoz. While wiring that he will not be reappointed, he evidently has not given up all hope, for his supporters were working yesterday for further endorsements, which were sent last evening by wire.

It is stated that Tom Powers, proprietor of the Coney Island saloon and gambling house, who is in Washington with Garrett, wired to his friends to get all the endorsements possible and they got to work. N. G. Buchoz, chief deputy collector, and Chas. Kinne, secretary of the civil service board and chief clerk in the custom house, were the principal workers, and were able last evening, through their day's efforts to telegraph a long string of endorsements for their chief.

It is said that the banks all signed the endorsement and that a number of the business men and most all the Democratic county officials also signed it.

Mr. Garrett, it is said, did not wire personally for the endorsements, simply sending a telegram that he was out of the race; that the President had declined to reappoint him, but Powers is said to have sent the telegram urging more endorsements, in the hope, that it would do some good and the President might reconsider.

Probable Cause.

"It's no use doing any more; the Powers incident at San Antonio is what finished that," said one of his closest friends today. That is the general opinion—that Mr. Roosevelt declined to reappoint Garrett to the position because of the incident when Garrett took Powers to the President's table for dinner at the Rough Rider reunion.

He has taken Powers to Washington with him. This was not considered policy, but he declined to listen to the importunities of his closest friends and advisors.

Mr. Garrett's term will expire on Jan. 2, and before that time the President probably will name his successor, who, it now appears will be Mr. Sharpe.

Mr. Sharpe is a business man at Clint, in this county, and has been identified actively with the Republican party for several years. Last year he was elected to the state legislature from this district in opposition to Pat Dwyer, the Democratic nominee, and is at present one of the two Republicans in the state legislature.

He is the author of the anti-gambling injunction law of Texas, which the Citizens League is now bringing into use against the gamblers in El Paso and did other good service for his constituency. He is the nominee of the El Paso County Republican organization for the place which he is now about to be named to fill.

Refuses To Give List.

When Numa P. Buchoz, chief deputy collector, was asked this afternoon for a list of those who endorsed Pat Garrett for reappointment, he refused to give the list or any information connected with the matter, saying he did not care to discuss it.

Now it became President Roosevelt's tiresome duty to answer the many letters from Garrett's supporters, explaining his reasons for not reappointing Pat. In each case he denied what everyone (then and now) refused to believe—that the Tom Powers incident was the cause of Garrett's downfall. Typical was this letter that the President sent to Emerson Hough:

December 16, 1905

Mr. Emerson Hough
First National Bank Building
Chicago, Illinois.

My dear Mr. Hough:

I have your letter of the 14th instant. The Secretary of the Treasury reported very strongly against Garrett's reappointment on the ground that he was an inefficient collector; that he was away a large part of the time from his office; that he was in debt and that his habits were bad.

This Colt Thunderer (serial number 138671) was presented to Pat Garrett by his friends at the El Paso Customs office in 1902. (Courtesy of Dr. Richard Marohn.)

The incident you mention had nothing to do with these reports; although it was an annoying matter to have Garrett bring up as his intimate friend a man who, however good a fellow he was, was well known as a professional gambler, and then have myself, Garrett and the gambler taken in a photograph together.

You will admit that it was not a happy incident, taking into account the fact that there are a good many different kinds of constituents in the United States. But I shall have a careful investigation of his office made by some thoroughly reliable man and abide by the result.

I appointed Garrett simply as a personal matter, and I must say that I have had a great deal of protest from some of the most respectable citizens in Texas and New Mexico, both in connection with his appointment and service.

I am not in the least sensitive to the past career of one of these Vikings of the border. I do not mind at all Garrett having killed four men. I think he was justified in killing them; but I do expect that in the present any man whom I appoint shall act right up to the handle.

With great regard, believe me,

Sincerely yours,

THEODORE ROOSEVELT

Unfortunately, Hough got the mistaken impression from this letter that Garrett still had a chance. On his way back to El Paso, Pat stopped off in Chicago and asked Hough to make an eleventh-hour appeal for him. What Hough did was to concoct an incredible letter, complete with two "exhibits." The effect of these missives, had it not already been too late, would probably have done more harm than good:

Emerson Hough
First National Bank Bldg.
Chicago

December 19, 1905.

Hon. Theodore Roosevelt,
Washington, D. C.

Dear Mr. President:

I prize your letter of December 16th, and shall not presume on it further than to say how glad I am you are going to give Garrett's Collectorship an investigation.

Possibly, since I am somewhat familiar with El Paso, you will see fit to place before Secretary Shaw a few things which I know to be facts, and which I have marked "Exhibit A" enclosed herewith. Perhaps you yourself may be personally interested in my "Exhibit B," on Tom Powers.

I wish I could lessen your very just annoyance at the San Antonio incident. The San Antonio men did not protect the President as a public man so much as they might have done. At the banquet at the Menger Hotel in the evening there was present Billy Sims (sic), a gambler of San Antonio. I know Sims a little. He and his men killed Ben Thompson in the theatre, while Thompson's hands were held by Coy, a big Mexican.[2]

I believe the Powers exhibit will show a cleaner record than that. Whatever your breadth and charity in personal view, your hosts and friends ought to have protected you better in your public capacity.

Garrett is here with me now, but I am not writing at his request, and hold no brief for him. I do so because he is sick and broken-hearted, not over the loss of his place but over the loss of your confidence in him, which he prized above all things.

As you know, these big outdoor men are childlike in some respects. Garrett's earlier training left him largely in ignorance of the term strict business, and this is the real apology for any shortcomings on his part. I believe your investigation will prove this.

If you can reappoint Pat Garrett, you will save his self-respect, and win the life devotion of himself and his many friends. If you will do this, I will promise you that Garrett's resignation shall come to you by July 1st of 1906, or at any time before that or after that which you will privately or publicly designate.

This I should like to see done, because I do not like to see the record of so straight a man clouded in any way. I don't think Garrett would go back into politics after that, but would return to his ranch, for a time at least.

Abraham Lincoln once pardoned a soldier sentenced to death for sleeping on picket. I do not wish to be impertinent, or mix in matters where I do not belong, but I do believe that if you can pardon Garrett for a dereliction which jeopardized no one but himself, you will never have occasion to regret it. If you put him back in this office, he would have to take it and would have to leave it at what you thought the proper time.

I am something of a gambler myself. A few months ago, I bet three hundred dollars with a man that the President would not back down from his attitude in railroad legislation. I am going to win that money and take it away from him. He is a Republican and so have I been all my life, and my father before me so long as there was a Republican party.

If you leave it to Western men, you will have to take a third term. I do not believe you know how much the country loves you and believes in you, and God knows they need something these days to believe in. It is far more important, in my private belief, for you to give back America to Americans, than it is even to give the Republican party back to the politicians.

If there had not been one name at the head of the ticket at the last election, a good many of us Western men wouldn't have known how to vote. You see, I am not very much of a politician; and neither am I in the habit of addressing letters to public men.

I thank you, dear Mr. President, for your kindness.

Respectfully Yours,

EMERSON HOUGH

With his letter, Emerson Hough sent the following two "exhibits":

EXHIBIT A

In Re Pat Garrett, Collector of Customs, El Paso.

Born in Louisiana. Moved to Buffalo Range and ranch country while a boy. Reached Fort Sumner, February, 1879. At different times Sheriff of Lincoln, Chavez and Dona Ana Counties, N. M.

Killed and drove out outlaws of eastern New Mexico and established law.

A man of little book education, but well born and of high sense of honor; largely known as a square man in Southwest. Not intemperate but drinks. Never have seen him show liquor and do not believe any one has.

There is no gambling room upstairs in El Paso, so far as Garrett knows. Garrett has not gambled, except that he played cards with Dr. Anderson and two other friends one night within the present year.

Occasionally goes into saloons but does not loaf there and does not frequent gambling places, open or private. Rooms at the house of Dr. Anderson above mentioned. Has many enemies, many of whom are in the Republican party at El Paso. Has a large personal following and endorsement of very many business men.

Is in debt, amount probably about $1500, as ascertained from his friends. Is one of the few collectors at El Paso who ever stayed in debt very long!

Lacks strict business training, but does not lack high sense of duty. Takes siesta of a few minutes at his room every day after lunch and has done so all his life; is then away from his office.

Owns a small ranch near San Andreas Mountains, about eighty miles north of El Paso, and a few months ago moved his family there. Has been up to see his family a few times. Was this fall with the undersigned in New Mexico for nearly three weeks, but this was the fault of the undersigned, who was in search of records of the old days and could get them in no other way. Do not believe that Garrett is in the habit of absenting himself from his duties.

Know that he is not a drunkard and not a gambler. Know that he is courteous to business men, and know that he is absolutely honest. From the start, he has been assailed by certain politicians of some prominence.

Undersigned is thoroughly familiar with El Paso and knows of only one sort of indiscretion of which Garrett has been guilty. This has nothing to do with his integrity. Would rather not state this but can do so if necessary.

Undersigned was born in Iowa and graduated at the State University of Iowa in 1880. Has never held public office nor asked for it in any form. Votes Republican ticket but is not a very good Republican these days. Lives in Chicago and has no interest whatever at El Paso. Lived in New Mexico 1882-84 and knew Garrett since then.

EXHIBIT B

In Re Tom Powers

Keeps saloon in El Paso. Does not now have gambling rooms, and has not had for a year and a half. Obeyed the law and took out even slot machines. Will be a candidate for Sheriff next year.

Was mayor of Colorado City, Tex., also deputy City Marshal. Killed City Marshal of Colorado City, after former had fired two shots at him; acquitted.

Is considered a game man. Assaulted by a race-track man and struck from behind with club. Refused to give up his gun to officer who came for him, but on learning his assailant was a prisoner, gave up his gun, and declined to interfere with him.

Can refer to following men as friends and vouchers:

Capt. Bill McDonald, Company B, State Rangers, who was with President Roosevelt on his hunt in Indian Nations.[3]

S. B. Burnett, on the same hunt, for whom Powers worked while a boy.

Congressman W. R. Smith, West district of Texas.

Congressman John S. Stephens, Northern District of Texas.

Congressmen Culbertson and Bailey of Texas and Smith of Arizona; also a member from the fifth congressional district of Texas; also Albert S. Burleson, of Austin, Tex.; also E. Spencer Blackburn, Member from South Carolina.

Was guest in New York Club of Dr. Elon N. Carpenter, 110 West 114th Street, New York City; also of F. W. Browersons, and I think also of W. C. Greene, copper magnate.[4]

Powers in his life has done the best he could, as have many Western men. Is a rough-and-ready sort, not prepossessing in personal appearance, but known as square and game. Once mortgaged his home to help a friend out of a tight place.

Main facts of above correct, and I think names correct. Powers does not know of this communication, of course.

EMERSON HOUGH

Dec. 19, 1905

NOTES

1. While this writer believes that the Powers incident in San Antonio was a contributing factor in Garrett's fate, I also believe that it may not have become the major factor had not Garrett compounded the offense by bringing Tom Powers to Washington with him—thus giving the anti-Roosevelt press a chance to rehash the incident anew. I feel it was this second blunder on Garrett's part that actually led to his removal.

2. On March 11, 1884, two noted gunfighters, Ben Thompson and John King Fisher, arrived by train in San Antonio. Word of their arrival had been telegraphed ahead to William H. "Billy" Simms and Joseph C. Foster, who had been partners with the late Jack Harris in San Antonio's Vaudeville Variety Theater. It was at this theater, on July 11, 1882, that Ben Thompson had shot and killed Harris. Thompson was acquitted of the killing on January 20, 1883.

Upon their March 11, 1884, arrival in San Antonio, Thompson and Fisher took in a performance of *Lady Audley's Secret*, and then proceeded to Gallagher's Saloon. From there they proceeded to—of all places—the Vaudeville Variety Theater, where Thompson promptly got into an argument with Joseph C. Foster. Standing nearby was an employee of the Vaudeville named Jacob Coy.

Suddenly, a volley of rifle and shotgun fire rang out and Thompson and Fisher crumpled to the floor. It was estimated that, together, the two men had been shot no less than twenty-four times. Joseph C. Foster was mortally wounded while a Vaudeville employee named Jacob Coy suffered a flesh wound.

Although the coroner's verdict stated that Ben Thompson's and King Fisher's deaths were caused by "pistols held and fired from the hands of J. C. Foster and Jacob Coy," it quickly became apparent that both gunmen were actually the victims of a well-orchestrated assassination plot. No one, then or now, seems comfortable with the coroner's verdict of "justifiable homicide" since all evidence points to a well-rehearsed ambush.

Whereas the coroner reported that Thompson was struck only four times, the autopsy listed eight bullets in Thompson's body—five of them in the head!

No autopsy was performed on King Fisher, but Charles H. Barnes, a reporter for the San Antonio *Express*, who also moonlighted as a clerk for the coroner, reported that the total number of wounds on both men numbered between 22 and 24! Some of these wounds were the result of buckshot. In addition, several of the bullets recovered from the bodies came from Winchester rifles.

Clearly, Ben Thompson and King Fisher were assassinated. The one question that will never be answered is just what role—if any—King Fisher played in the plot that led to the bloody events of March 11, 1884. It is known, for example, that King Fisher was friendly with both Joseph C. Foster and Jack Harris, as well as Billy Simms. Had he set Thompson up—only to be double-crossed by his pals? Or was King Fisher just the proverbial innocent bystander? At this late date, it's doubtful we'll ever know for certain.

3. William Jesse "Bill" McDonald was born on September 28, 1852, in Kemper County, Mississippi. McDonald served as commander of Company B, Texas Rangers, from January, 1891, until January 19, 1907. During April, 1905, Governor Lanham of Texas summoned McDonald and informed him that he had been selected to accompany President Theodore Roosevelt and his party on a wolf hunt in Comanche County, Oklahoma. McDonald was less than thrilled.

"Governor," McDonald said, "you know I'm a hell-roarin' Democrat, and don't care much for Republican Presidents in general and this one in particular. I'd rather you picked another man for the job."

McDonald was informed that he had no choice, and would have to make the best of it. When McDonald and Roosevelt first met on a train bound for the Panhandle, the dialogue, according to his 1909 biography (*Captain Bill McDonald, Texas Ranger: A Story of Frontier Reform*, by Albert Bigelow Paine, pages 274-275), went this way:

"Look here," he (Roosevelt) said, you were introduced to me as Captain McDonald; you're not Captain Bill McDonald of the Rangers, are you?"

Captain Bill nodded.

"That's my name, Mr. President," he said, "I've been captain of a company of Rangers for a long time.

"Is it possible? Well, I've heard a good deal about you."

Captain Bill smiled, as who wouldn't.

"Why, Mr. President," he said, "I didn't think you'd ever heard about the Rangers."

The President's teeth shone in expansive appreciation.

"Yes, indeed I have, and I've heard all about you."

Bill McDonald went on to become President Woodrow Wilson's bodyguard. Later, Wilson appointed McDonald United States Marshal for the Northern District of Texas. McDonald was still serving in that post when he contracted pneumonia and died on January 15, 1918, at age sixty-five.

4. "Copper magnate" though he might have been, William C. Greene was not the best witness Hough could have come up with for Tom Powers. On July 1, 1897, Greene shot and killed James Burnett at Tombstone, Arizona's O. K. Corral. Despite the fact that Burnett was killed in cold blood, a jury returned a "not guilty" verdict on December 20, 1897.

J. C. Lea of Roswell, New Mexico, was one of the state's most powerful men in the 1880's as an industrialist, capitalist, and railroad magistrate. (Courtesy of the Fulton Collection, University of Arizona Archives.)

Ash Upson assisted Pat Garrett in writing THE AUTHENTIC LIFE OF BILLY THE KID. He was probably Garrett's closest friend. (Courtesy of the Fulton Collection, University of Arizona Archives.)

Chapter 12

GARRETT STEPS DOWN

Emerson Hough's well-intended (albeit unintentionally comical) effort came too late in the game. Before his letter (and "exhibits") even reached Washington, the decision was final and Garrett's successor had been chosen. The El Paso *Herald* of December 20, 1905, gave this account of the event:

HON. A. L. SHARPE'S NOMINATION FOR CUSTOMS COLLECTOR CONFIRMED BY SENATE

WASHINGTON, D. C. Dec. 20.—President Roosevelt this afternoon sent to the senate the nomination of Alfred L. Sharpe to be customs collector at El Paso, replacing Pat. F. Garrett, whose term has expired.

The senate in executive session immediately confirmed the nomination and Mr. Sharpe will return at once to El Paso to take charge of the office immediately after the holidays.

That same issue of the *Herald* also gave an account of Garrett's meeting with President Roosevelt some nine days earlier. Once again, the Tom Powers incident in San Antonio was given as the real cause for Garrett's failure to be reappointed:

PAT GARRETT'S WHITE HOUSE VISIT

Washington Papers Say His Reception Was Cold.

Blame Tom Powers.

The first Washington papers containing anything on the visit of Pat Garrett, El Paso's Collector of Customs, to the White House to see the President in the interest of reappointment, have been received. The Washington *Times*, of the 15th (last Friday), says:

"Pat" Garrett, the slayer of "Billy the Kid," has been turned

down cold and hard by the President in his application for reappointment as Collector of Customs at El Paso. Garrett's term expires on
Dec. 19, and he was here Monday to see the President about another
term. But the President coldly said "Nay."

P. F. Garrett is a famous character in and around El Paso. Garrett
was a personal friend of the President. For years he was Sheriff of
Lincoln County, New Mexico, and it was while in this office that he
shot and killed the celebrated "Billy the Kid."

The trouble with Garrett, it is said, is that he offended the President by taking a professional gambler and saloon keeper with him to
the Rough Rider's reunion at San Antonio, last spring. The President
is said to have resented this action, and treated Garrett with great
coolness when he called at the White House Monday.

It was thought that "Pat" would get the appointment for the asking of it, but when he left the executive mansion he wore a very
gloomy expression, and would not talk to the newspaper men.

He has a good record as a collector and his only offense is that he
took Tom Powers, the gambler, of El Paso, with him to the President's
reception at San Antonio.

The *Post* of the 16th (Saturday), says:

Long, lean, and eagle-eyed "Pat" Garrett, whose six feet and four
inches make him look about three inches thick, Collector of Customs
at El Paso, Tex., who has been in this city for four or five days, will
probably not be reappointed to the office he now holds.

Garrett killed "Billy the Kid," but he has lost standing with the
political contingent that stood for his appointment four years ago,
and the sliding board, it is believed, is ready for him.

Ever since his interview with President Roosevelt a few days ago
he has been dejected. He no longer tries to watch all the doors open-
ing into the rotunda of the New Willard, as if looking for the man
trying to get the drop on him, and in other ways he shows the bitterness of defeat.

It is intimated that the coldness at the White House was increased
by the fact that he took with him to the Rough Rider reunion last
spring a saloon keeper and gambler who had never smelled gun-
powder, except in a barroom brawl.

With no hope left, Pat Garrett started the long journey
back to El Paso. The El Paso *Herald* of December 21, 1905, announced that both the present and future collectors were due in
shortly:

RETIRING AND INCOMING COLLECTORS

A telegram last night from A. L. Sharpe, the newly appointed Customs Collector, confirmed the *Herald's* exclusive announcement that he had been appointed and confirmed as Collector of Customs at El Paso, and said, "Smith and I are feeling good."

He did not say when they would return home, but a telegram from J. A. Smith announced that he would arrive Sunday afternoon on Golden State Limited No. 43. It is presumed that Mr. Sharpe will arrive with him as Mrs. Sharpe is sick and a telegram has been sent informing him of her illness.

Retiring Collector Pat Garrett is expected to return home Sunday on the Santa Fe.

The day after this item appeared, President Roosevelt wrote Emerson Hough and expanded on his reasons for not reappointing Garrett. In doing so, he compared the deposed Garrett to two other White House Gunfighters:

December 22, 1905

Mr. Emerson Hough
First National Bank Building
Chicago, Illinois

My dear Mr. Hough:

I am very sorry to have to write you that I can not reappoint Pat. I sent your last letter to the Secretary saying that I wanted to reappoint Pat unless it was out of the question, and I wanted an investigation to show me that it was out of the question.

The Secretary came down at once with the full reports of the investigation by his department and with one of the men who made the investigation. They showed a very poor state of affairs and they placed me so that I either had to give up any attempt to secure good service under the Secretary of the Treasury or let Pat go.

I simply can not take the position of playing favorites once a man is in office, for if I do I immediately lose my power of demanding efficiency and honesty in the public service. For example, I have just removed an assistant treasurer in Pennsylvania who was backed heartily by Senator Penrose. I have just removed a marshal and a district attorney in Nebraska who were backed heartily by the entire Nebraska delegation.

I am refusing to reappoint man after man who I think is inefficient. If under these circumstances I make an exception for a personal
favorite, I deprive myself of all standing and make the men who are
only too willing to grumble anyhow, certain that I am insincere.

This is a very hard thing for me to write you because I like you
and believe in you. But I want you to understand that Pat Garrett
was my personal choice, just, for instance, as Seth Bullock[1] in Deadwood and Ben Daniels in Arizona,[2] both of whom are much of the
Pat Garrett stamp, are my personal choices. But if the Department of
Justice finds that either of these men does not do his duty, why, he
will have to go.

Faithfully Yours,

THEODORE ROOSEVELT

Pat Garrett arrived in El Paso almost four years to the very
day he had made his triumphal return, after gaining his appointment, in 1901. This time there were no cheering crowds, just a
small group of friends and several curious reporters. The Christmas issue of the El Paso *Herald* offered this brief account of
Garrett's return:

SHARPE AND GARRETT BOTH HOME

Pat Garrett, the retiring Customs Collector, accompanied by Tom
Powers returned yesterday afternoon on the delayed T. & P. train, and
A. L. Sharpe, the newly appointed collector, returned shortly after
midnight on the delayed Golden State Limited, both arriving home in
time for Christmas.

Mr. Sharpe left this morning for his home at Clint.

J. A. Smith says that he is very happy as a result of the success
they had in their fight for the collectorship.

"Credit is due to every man who helped us," said he this morning,
"and no special man deserves the credit for landing the office for a
home man."

The following day—Tuesday, December 26, 1905—the El
Paso *Herald* gave a far more detailed account of Garrett's return
home. Once again, Pat was emphatic in claiming that Tom
Powers was not the cause for his removal:

POWERS DID NOT CAUSE HIM TO LOSE JOB

Pat Garrett Says It Was Due to Shaw's Antagonism—Declares
Powers to Be Better Than His Detractors.

Customs Collector Pat Garrett, who returned Sunday from Washington and New York, accompanied by Tom Powers, denies that the Powers incident at San Antonio and the fact that he was accompanied to Washington by Powers, had anything to do with the President's failure to reappoint him to office and says it was due solely to Secretary Shaw that he was not reappointed; that the Secretary protested at his reappointment and the President did not like to antagonize a cabinet officer by naming him. Said Mr. Garrett:

"The President did mention the Powers matter and said that the newspaper references to my having taken Powers to dine with him at San Antonio had fretted him, but he further said: 'Mr. Garrett, Secretary Shaw does not want you reappointed; he protests against it and I cannot name you for another term.'

"I did not apologize to the President for going to San Antonio with Powers, but told him that I would introduce Tom Powers to anybody.

"And right here I will say that Tom Powers is a better man than any of those who have been making this talk against him and this goes for anybody. There is not a man in El Paso who is more charitable or will do more for the welfare of the town, or who is a truer friend than Tom Powers.

"When I called on Secretary Shaw at Washington I saw at once that he was not going to stand for my reappointment if he could help it. He said that I had been discourteous and abrupt to the people having business with my office and that on the whole my reappointment was opposed by all of the best people here.

"I told him that 99 percent of the people having business with my office were satisfied with its conduct and asked him if my collections had not always been all right and if I had not always enforced the law.

"He acknowledged that I had handled the office honestly, but said the objections raised against me came from so many people that he could not and would not recommend my reappointment. I do not know who made the objections, but anyhow, I was not reappointed and it was because of the antagonism of Secretary Shaw.

"The Secretary said he was reliably informed that I gambled and that I owed a lot of unpaid bills. I suppose those who were opposing me, made the complaints to the Secretary before I reached Washington."

The following in the Houston *Chronicle* from Fort Worth is inter-esting in connection with Mr. Garrett's feelings regarding his turn down:

"I cheerfully acquiesce in the President's action in not reappoint-ing me," said Pat Garrett to the *Chronicle* correspondent today.

"I not only acquiesce, but endorse the President's action, for the reason that I am of the opinion that he did the proper thing in the premises. The President said he could not appoint men when one of his cabinet, Secretary Shaw, objected.

"I am not disgruntled in the least, and have nothing but the best feelings for President Roosevelt, who I regard as the greatest man in the world, without exception."

Garrett will hereafter live on his ranch in New Mexico.

J. A. Smith Talks.

J. A. Smith was seen this morning and asked if he had preferred any charges against Mr. Garrett either before he went to Washington or after he arrived, and he declared emphatically that he had not and said the only fight he made on Mr. Garrett was that he did not affili-ate with and encourage the Republican Party in El Paso, and that the place should go to a man who belonged here and affiliated with the local organization. Continuing he said:

"Not a single paper was filed, either by myself or Mr. Sharpe, either with the President or Secretary of the Treasury, nor were we parties to anything that might have been filed.

"The Secretary had reports from two special agents who had been in El Paso making investigations, and it was from these that he made the charges against Mr. Garrett in their interview. I never furnished these special agents with one word against Mr. Garrett.

"I have never furnished any special agent with anything against Mr. Garrett, but one report to the secretary about two years ago even censured me as favoring Mr. Garrett because he had appointed rela-tives of my wife to positions under him."[3]

The same day that this article appeared, Emerson Hough typed a letter to Pat Garrett, telling the former Collector of Customs what he already knew:

December 26, 1905.

Dear Pat:

I have another letter from President Roosevelt, and our guess is right. You lose out. The President is mighty nice in his letter, and speaks of you as Pat and with affection.

We both know that he personally would like to see you in, and we both know the reason, political and departmental, why he does not reappoint you. This much I can say without violating any confidence of his. His decision was made on the report of Secretary Shaw, who, for reasons of his own, is strongly against you.

Personally, I think this the luckiest thing that could happen to you. Working for a salary is like a horse following a bunch of hay tied in front of his nose. It looks good but the horse never quite gets it.

With your ranch and town site and book work, I reckon the Lord will take care of you some how. I hope you get home safe and are all right.

Yours sincerely,

EMERSON HOUGH

Pat Garrett served his last day as Collector of Customs on January 2, 1906. On that day he turned the reins of power over to A. L. Sharpe. The El Paso *Herald* of January 3, 1906, reported the event this way:

A. L. SHARPE TAKES CHARGE OF CUSTOM HOUSE

New Collector Takes Oath of Office and Assumes the
Duties As Collector Of the Port.

A. L. Sharpe is now the Collector of Customs of the El Paso district. He took the official oath Tuesday afternoon and assumed responsibility for the office at 6 o'clock in the evening, taking charge of the day's cash and becoming actually responsible for its conduct for the day, thus officially assuming the office at the beginning of the first day of the new year and quarter.

This morning Mr. Sharpe began checking over the contents of the federal building of which he becomes custodian, and will put in the day at this work, and will probably then not finish the task, as he has to receipt to the retiring collector, Garrett, for every piece of furniture in the building, down to the chairs, the official seals, etc.

Mr. Sharpe, the new collector, has lived in Texas the past 24 years, and this is his first federal position. His first public position of any kind was that of representative to the state legislature for this district, to which he was elected in November, 1904.

The new collector was born in Ravena, Ohio, a little over 47 years ago, or in the latter part of the year 1858; he resided in Ohio until he grew to manhood and for several years afterward, until he came to Texas in 1882.

Mr. Sharpe entered the railroad service when a young man, going with the Cleveland, Lorraine & Wheeling road in Ohio and remaining with this road until he moved to Texas 24 years ago, when he went with the I. & G. N. (then a part of the Missouri Pacific system) with the passenger department, first at San Antonio and later at Georgetown.

In 1892 Mr. Sharpe left the railroad and went into the mercantile business at Georgetown, where he reamined until five years ago, when he moved to El Paso establishing himself at Clint, in this county, where he has lived and conducted his business for two and a half years past.

NOTES

1. Seth Bullock was born on July 24, 1847, in Sandwich, Ontario, Canada. Bullock left Canada in 1869 and moved to Montana, where he soon became a member of the Territorial Senate. One of Bullock's resolutions called for the Congress of the United States to set aside the Yellowstone country as a National Park. Seth's resolution was adopted by the legislature, and Yellowstone Park was established by federal statute on March 1, 1872.

Bullock was elected Sheriff of Lewis and Clark County on August 4, 1873. A date of more enduring value was September 14, 1874, when Bullock married a schoolteacher named Martha Eccles in Salt Lake City. The marriage lasted until Seth's death and produced three children.

Seth Bullock arrived in Deadwood on August 1, 1876, just one day before Wild Bill Hickok was assassinated there. The following year Seth was elected as the first sheriff of Lawrence County, with headquarters in Deadwood. Like many sheriffs in the old west, Seth also held a concurrent Deputy U. S. Marshal's commission, allowing him to extend his man-hunting beyond the jurisdiction of Lawrence County.

During 1879 Bullock moved farther north in the Dakota Territory and, with a partner named Sol Star, established the Star and

Bullock Stock Farm—soon known simply as the SB Ranch. It was while Bullock was engaged in his ranching endeavor, that an unlikely character made his appearance in the Dakota Territory during June of 1884. He was a myopic young New Yorker named Theodore Roosevelt. The recently-widowed Roosevelt had left his infant daughter in the care of friends, and headed west to establish a life as a rancher in the Badlands of the Dakota Territory. Thus began the lifelong love affair between Theodore Roosevelt and the people of the old west.

In his 1913 autobiography (pages 130-131) Theodore Roosevelt devoted considerable space to his first meeting with Seth Bullock and recalled that:

> Later, Seth Bullock became, and has ever since remained, one of my staunchest and most valued friends. He served as Marshal for South Dakota under me as President. When, after the close of my term, I went to Africa, on getting back to Europe I cabled Seth Bullock to bring over Mrs. Bullock and meet me in London, which he did; by that time I felt that I just had to meet my own people, who spoke my neighborhood dialect.

Seth Bullock's last act of devotion to Theodore Roosevelt began within a month after Teddy's death on January 6, 1919. Bullock (who was himself dying from cancer) convinced the Black Hills Society of Pioneers to erect a monument to Roosevelt on Sheep Mountain, located close to Deadwood. The peak was renamed Mount Roosevelt and a tower constructed on it was officially dedicated on July 4, 1919, during ceremonies presided over by Seth Bullock and General Leonard Wood.

Seth Bullock lost his battle to cancer on September 23, 1919, at the age of seventy-two. He died at his residence at 28 Van Buren Street in Deadwood. He was buried in Mount Moriah cemetery, not far from the graves of Wild Bill Hickok and Calamity Jane.

2. The career of Benjamin Franklin Daniels as one of Theodore Roosevelt's "White House Gunfighters," was briefly described in the first volume of this trilogy (*Masterson and Roosevelt*) and will be covered completely in the third and final volume, which is devoted to Daniels.

3. Apparently the passing of thirteen months had altered J. A. Smith's opinion of Pat Garrett more than somewhat—as is obvious from this letter:

El Paso, Texas.
November 5th., 1904.

Honorable Leslie M. Shaw,
Secretary of the Treasury,
Washington, D. C.

My dear Mr. Secretary:

While acting in the capacity of Private Secretary for Honorable R. B. Hawley, of Texas, and in accordance with instructions given me, I made a number of statements regarding the character and career of Honorable Patrick Garrett, Collector of the Port of El Paso, Texas, which statements, I find, after sojourning in El Paso for some months, to be utterly false and untrue.

I think, it is due Mr. Garrett that I write you the truth.

I have seen Mr. Garrett repeatedly while I have been in El Paso, and never saw him under the influence of liquor, nor has he the appearance of a man who drinks. He impresses me as being a gentleman in every sense of the word—thoroughly competent to conduct the affairs of his office.

Above all, Mr. Garrett tells the truth, which I regret to say few men in this part of the country appear able to do—especially does this apply to several of Mr. Garrett's accusers—local Republicans here in El Paso, who not only do not speak the truth, but are not honest, which statement I make from personal dealings with the gentlemen.

With regard to Mr. Garrett being a professional gambler, I do not think there is any truth in this charge. Mr. Garrett, I understand, plays cards—but here in the south, the majority of gentlemen play cards.

Mr. Garrett does not identify himself with the local Republican organization in El Paso, and I believe his position in the matter is a correct one. The Republicans here devote their time and energy to fighting each other.

There is absolutely no hope for the Republican party in the State of Texas. It has a great future in New Mexico, and Mr. Garrett's identification with the Republican party in New Mexico rather than in Texas, is a much more logical and proper attitude than to be mixed up with a lot of people, whose only party ambition is federal patronage.

I realize now, since coming to El Paso, that President Roosevelt, in the appointment of Mr. Garrett—made a most wise selection—not only because of the recognition of the Republican

Bat Masterson as he appeared when he was thirty-two years old.

party in New Mexico, but Mr. Garrett is a man worthy of the trust reposed in him.

It affords me great pleasure to be able to write you this letter, as I feel, in the interest of justice, it should be written.

With assurances of highest esteem, believe me,

Faithfully yours,

J. A. SMITH

The site of Pat Garrett's murder outside of Las Cruces near the Organ Mountains as it appears today. (Courtesy James H. Powell.)

Chapter 13

THE MURDER OF PATRICK FLOYD GARRETT

With little else to distract him, Pat Garrett's thoughts once again turned to the book project he was assisting Emerson Hough with. Hough responded to a letter from Pat with this request for information:

January 6, 1906.

Hon. P. F. Garrett,
El Paso, Texas.

Dear Pat:

I am now working on the book. I wish you would answer the following questions:

(1) What was the name of your Mexican deputy who killed the prisoner you were trying to take near Las Cruces?

(2) What was the name of the sheriff who was after that prisoner from the Indian Nations?

(3) What was the name of the man with the red spot in his eye you took near Fort Sumner?

(4) Who can tell me anything about Sam Bass, the Texas desperado?

You may hand this letter to Tom Powers and ask him to tell me, if he can, where Bass was born, how old he was when killed, where killed, and under what circumstances; also how many crimes, murders, etc., he had committed.

The book opens up well before me and I think will be worth doing, and I want to do it as well as I know. Hoping everything is going well with you,

Yours sincerely,

EMERSON HOUGH

Garrett's reply is not included among Hough's papers, but apparently Pat tried to look the writer up in Chicago—as is evident from this letter:

February 7, 1906.

Mr. Pat F. Garrett,
El Paso, Texas.

Dear Pat:

My servant tells me that last Saturday you telephoned my house while I was away. I do not find any other notice of your having been in town, and confess it looks a little like a cold deal.

I have not had any answer, and shall be glad to know your post office address, as there may be matters connected with the issuance of this book which will make it desirable for me to hear from you.

Yours sincerely,

EMERSON HOUGH

Garrett replied to Hough on March 8, 1906, and admitted that he had indeed been in Chicago but failed to make contact with the writer. Pat never did say why he wanted to see Hough but concluded his letter with this interesting line:

You will please pardon the unintelligent manner in which this letter is written from the fact that I am suffering great distress of mind and soul.[1]

This "distress of mind and soul" would remain Pat Garrett's constant companion until the day he died—which was less than two years away.

As always, Pat was beset with financial miseries. After leaving El Paso, Pat returned to New Mexico where he held title to two ranches. Garrett had mortgaged both of these properties for $3,567 to raise much-needed cash. When Garrett failed to exhibit any inclination to repay these loans, the creditors

Pat Garrett (tallest man) with his friends at Torrance, New Mexico, when they were traveling to George Curry's inauguration in Santa Fe on August 8, 1907. (Courtesy of William A. Keleher.)

quickly closed in. It ended on September 4, 1906, when the county auctioned off all of Garrett's personal possessions to satisfy the judgements against him. The total came to a pathetic $650.

In addition to Pat's other troubles, Emerson Hough decided to switch publishers. Hough's book (*The Story of the Outlaw*) was being printed by the Outing Publishers, who changed the format around to such an extent that Garrett's contribution became all but worthless. Garrett did receive an advance of $200—but with the understanding that it would be refunded if the book failed to sell. That $200 appears to be the only money Pat Garrett ever made from his long collaboration with Emerson Hough.

When Garrett next contacted Hough, it was—rather predictably—to hit him up for some cash:

Organ N. Mex
February 7 1907

Dear Mr. Hough

Your favor to (illegible) and find us enjoying the best of health. We are on the same little ranch where you saw us last. Been trying to (illegible) some improvements (illegible) to plant about one and 1/2 acres in garden last year and it proved to be such a good one we have big hopes for this year.

I never saw such fine vegetables and mellons grown any where in my life as we have here.

We have sufficient water, and our range prospects were never as good as this spring. Have had a very mild winter with a great deal of rain, for the last ten days we have had the finest Spring weather you ever saw.

You speak of money. Well suppose you are doing well in a financial way, the opposite has been the case with me. Everything seems to go wrong with me.

I was sold out last fall by the Sheriff. Went on a note with a friend was such judgement obtained execution is here, but we have our ranch and a few stock left and I am going to stay here and build up again.

A little money would be worth a great deal to me at present to fix up the ranch, get a few more stock & do you think there is any chance to (illegible) my interest in the book with you, if you can see your way clear it would be a great favor to us.

The family are all well. Pauline is in your (illegible) and growing fast. They all appreciate your kind rememberance and send their best wish to you.

Yours

P. F. GARRETT

Emerson Hough responded to Pat's plea for financial aid by sending him a copy of *The Story of the Outlaw*. Hough went on to offer assistance in yet another of Garrett's irrigation schemes and offered the usual words of good cheer. Significantly, the one item that Hough did not offer was money:

George Curry served as a Captain in Roosevelt' Rough Riders and was Governor of the New Mexico Territory at the time of Garrett's murder in 1908.

Chicago,
February 12, 1907.

Hon. P. F. Garrett,
Organ, N. M.

Dear Pat:

I am sending you a copy of the book and copy of my letter to the publishers. I shall be sorry if anything about the work does not please you.

I had a great deal of trouble about doing this book; had to change its entire plan etc., had to stand delay from the publishers, and now I don't want any more little annoyances from it on their part, such as that I mention in my letter to them.

Now as this book is just out, and as it will be some time before I will get anything from it, and since as it stands you have had more out of it than I have, I think we had better let that rest for a while, and see if we can't dig something up for you from this artesian project.

I will keep after Prof. Curtis and put you in touch with his man as soon as I can.

I suspected something was wrong with you in a business way when I did not hear from you, but I am heartily sorry you got in such deep water. All I can say is, keep your nerve, for money is made quicker now than it ever was, and I have no doubt that it will come your way. When it does, nail it this time. I will do anything I can in the way of practical help.

With best regards to you all, sincerely

Yours,

EMERSON HOUGH

It was five months before Garrett wrote Hough again. This time his letter concerned *The Story of the Outlaw:*

Las Cruces, N. M.
July 2nd, 1907.

Mr. Emerson Hough,
1st National Bank Building,
Chicago, Ill.

Dear Mr. Hough:

No doubt you have me recorded as one of your most unfaithful correspondents, which I will admit that the chances are you are correct, therefore will not attempt to make any apology for not having answered your last letters.

I received copies of books sent by you also those sent by the Publishing Company. I have read the work and am well pleased with it as a whole, but there are some parts of it that are not up to what I expected. When I see you will discuss these points in detail.

I suppose, owing to the season of the year, you will hardly be able to do anything with our artesian water proposition until, perhaps October; in the meantime if you don't feel too much miffed you might write me and tell me about yourself and the good madam.

The weather is exceedingly warm and dry in this section at present, but we hope to have rain in a few days, when we will get back to our normal climatic conditions. Mrs. G. and the babies are all well, and send their regards to you and yours.

Yours truly,

P. F. GARRETT

Whether Hough took Garrett's comments as a personal rebuff is uncertain; whatever the case, Garrett's letter of July 2, 1907, terminated their known correspondence.

A fact all but unnoticed by Pat Garrett at this time was the leasing of his Bear Canyon Ranch, by his 21 year-old son, Dudley Poe Garrett, to a 31 year-old cowboy named Jesse Wayne Brazel. Pat attached no particular significance to this seemingly mundane transaction, which could only help out by providing some cash. Besides, Garrett had more important things on his mind . . . .

President Roosevelt had named Pat's long-time friend, George Curry,[2] to be the next Governor of the New Mexico Territory. Garrett met with Curry and was promised the post of Superintendent of the territorial prison in Santa Fe, once Curry was inaugurated. Once again, Pat Garrett had found an apparent savior when he needed one most—and, once again, his self-destruct switch went off.

Curry's inauguration was still a while off, and Garrett desperately needed cash in the meantime. Leaving his family in New Mexico, Garrett returned to El Paso where he accepted employment with H. M. Maple and Company, a real estate firm. Unfortunately, Garrett found little to interest him in real estate and spent most of his time with a certain "Mrs. Brown"—an El Paso prostitute with whom he set up housekeeping. When word of Garrett's escapades reached the ear of Governor-to-be Curry, Pat's promised appointment was promptly withdrawn.

On August 8, 1907, George Curry was inaugurated as Governor in Santa Fe. Curry invited some of the most prominent citizens of New Mexido to his inauguration. Pat Garrett was surprised, and touched, when Curry extended an invitation to him also.

Shortly after the Curry inauguration, Pat Garrett began having problems with Jesse Wayne Brazel. When Brazel signed his five-year lease, he indicated only that he would be raising "livestock." Garrett mistakenly assumed that the "livestock" would be either horses or cattle; instead Brazel began bringing in large herds of goats—which were an anathema to a cattleman like Pat Garrett.

The furious Garrett attempted to break the lease, alleging that he had a "verbal agreement" with Brazel which excluded goats. When Brazel denied this, the lawyers took over. As it happened, the carefully-worded contract omitted any mention of just how Brazel planned to use Garrett's land.

At this point, two key characters entered the drama; the first was Carl Adamson, and the other was a relative of Adamson's, by marriage, named Jim Miller.[3] Garrett met with Miller and Adamson in El Paso and explained his difficulties with Brazel. Miller offered to meet with Brazel, which Garrett agreed to.

When Brazel and Miller met, Wayne flatly refused to cancel his lease with Garrett unless a buyer could be found for his herd of twelve hundred goats. Miller quickly agreed to find a buyer and a contract was drawn up. Garrett thought his troubles were over and confidently returned to his ranch at Organ, New Mexico, on February 20, 1908.

Then the situation quickly turned around—Brazel claimed that he had somehow miscounted his herd, and that there were actually 1,800 goats rather than the 1,200 Brazel estimated earlier. Jim Miller seemed visibly disturbed by this news, telling the distraught Garrett that the entire deal would probably have to be called off. Deep in despair, Garrett promptly cabled his friend, Governor George Curry:

> I am in a hell of a fix. I have been trying to sell my ranch, but no luck. For God's sake send me fifty dollars.[4]

Curry quickly sent Garrett the check, which Pat planned to cash when he went to Las Cruces that coming Saturday—February 29, 1908.

On Friday, February 28, Carl Adamson arrived at the Garrett ranch. Something about Adamson's behavior made Pat's wife visibly nervous and she expressed her fears to Pat. Garrett told his wife not to worry; the following morning he would go to Las Cruces, cash Governor Curry's check, and also meet with Wayne Brazel. He expressed great hopes of being able to resolve his difficulties with Brazel.

Early in the morning of February 29, 1908, Pat Garrett bade farewell to his family and started for Las Cruces in a two-horse buggy, accompanied by Carl Adamson. About two miles from their destination, Garrett and Adamson came upon two horsemen on what was then called the Mail-Scott Road. One of the riders took off before he could be identified; the other remained for the approach of the buggy. It was Jesse Wayne Brazel.

Brazel rode alongside the buggy and was soon involved in a heated debate with Garrett over the goat issue. Garrett allegedly threatened to remove Brazel from his land somehow if the deal fell through. Near a spot called Alameda Arroyo, Carl Adamson halted the team, claiming that he had to answer a call of nature. Garrett saw nothing strange in the request, and decided that it would be a good time to relieve his own kidneys.

As Pat climbed down from the buggy, he took his Burgess folding shotgun with him. Pat cradled the weapon in his right arm while he unbuttoned his trousers with his left hand. Thus, it was while occupied in one of man's most basic functions that a bullet slammed into the back of Pat Garrett's head.

Shortly afterward, in nearby Las Cruces, Deputy Felipe Lucero was preparing his lunch when Jesse Wayne Brazel burst in exclaiming: "Lock me up. I've just killed Pat Garrett!"

NOTES

1. Cited in Metz, *Pat Garrett: The Story of a Western Lawman,* pages 280-281.
2. George Curry was born in Bayou Sara, Louisiana, on April 3, 1862. As a youth he went west and found employment as a cowboy.

During the November 1880 elections, 18 year-old Curry was a supporter of Pat Garrett in his race for Sheriff of Lincoln County, New Mexico. Then employed as manager of Lincoln County's Brock Ranch, Curry tried to interest other cowboys in supporting Garrett and thus ridding the territory of Billy the Kid.

One day a mysterious gunman rode into Curry's camp and listened while Curry expounded upon the wisdom of voting for Pat Garrett. After finishing his meal, the gunman said: "You are a good cook and a good fellow, but if you think Pat Garrett is going to carry this precinct for Sheriff, you are a damn poor politician!"

After the youthful gunman left, one of Curry's cowboys informed him that he had been discussing Pat Garrett's election with Billy the Kid!

Between 1888 and 1892, Curry served successively as county treasurer, clerk, and assessor for Lincoln County, New Mexico. Curry was elected Sheriff of Lincoln County (the same job he once helped Pat Garrett campaign for) in 1892 and served two years. Curry went on to serve in the New Mexico Territorial Senate from 1894 until 1896, serving his final year as President of that body. When the Spanish-American War commenced, Curry was appointed Captain of Troop H in the Rough Riders and formed a close friendship with Theodore Roosevelt.

Curry returned to New Mexico after the short war; when the new county of Otero was organized, George Curry became its first sheriff—serving between March and August, 1899. As sheriff, Curry conducted negotiations with the governor for the surrender of Fountain murder suspects Oliver Lee and Jim Gilliland.

During the Philippine Insurrection, Curry served as Captain of Troop K and commanded the regimental scouts between 1899-1901. Between April and August of 1901 Curry served as Governor of the Philippine province of Ambos Camarine. Following this, he served as Chief of Police in Manila. Following a stint as manager of the Camarine Mercantile Company, Curry served as governor of the Philippine province of Isabella in 1904-1905.

It was while serving as governor of the province of Samar (1905-1907) that Curry had his most legendary exploit. During a native insurrrection, Curry commanded a detachment of fifty-one troopers who were ambushed by a larger force of *insurrectos*. Only five men—including Curry—survived the battle. President Roosevelt took note of his former Rough Rider buddy's exploit by wiring him:

> Hearty congratulations on your miraculous escape. Keep a stiff upper lip. I am with you.
>
> Theodore

*Wayne Brazel
confessed to the
murder of Pat
Garrett. He posed for
this photograph after
shaving his head as a
lark. Jim Lee (left)
and Will Craven
posed with him.
(Courtesy of Hal
Cox.)*

After eight years in the Philippines, Curry grew homesick for New Mexico and lobbied to wrangle an appointment as Governor of the New Mexico Territory from his pal, President Theodore Roosevelt. On April 20, 1907, Roosevelt announced Curry's appointment, writing him on the same date that: "All I have to ask of you is that you give an absolutely honest and common-sense administration."

In order to appoint Curry, Roosevelt first had to dismiss the incumbent governor, Herbert J. Hagerman. Then, Roosevelt had to explain his position to many friends of the various "White House Gunfighters"—as he did in this July 27, 1907, note to Alfred Henry Lewis:

> When I turned Hagerman out I made up my mind that I would appoint a man who was absolutely straight and yet a real westerner. I accordingly appointed George Curry. You can find out all about him from Bat Masterson as he was one of Bat's deputies in the old days at Dodge City.

It is highly unlikely that George Curry ever knew Bat Masterson during the latter's term as Sheriff of Ford County, Kansas—which expired before Curry turned eighteen. Certainly, there is no evidence, and no record, of Curry having served as one of "Bat's deputies" there during that period. However, it is worthy of note that neither Curry nor Masterson ever did anything to discourage this oft-repeated fable.

Obviously, both had something to gain from the myth. For his part, Curry could add to his reputation by claiming to have been the deputy of a celebrated gunfighter. Masterson, on the other hand, could brag that the then Governor of the New Mexico Territory had once been his deputy. There is a possible, but not altogether satisfying, explanation that Masterson might have confused George Curry with an old gunfighting crony named Jim Currie. Since they had both sought, and won, appointments from their mutual friend, neither George Curry nor Bat Masterson had anything to loose by pretending that they had been close pals "in the old days at Dodge City." If Roosevelt suspected the truth, he never let on.

George Curry was inaugurated as Governor of the New Mexico Territory on August 8, 1907. Among the dignitaries in attendance were Pat Garrett and Albert Bacon Fall. Governor Curry had appointed Fall as his Attorney General. President Roosevelt violently opposed this appointment and made his position crystal-clear in a letter to Curry written on August 17, 1907:

> I do think it is important that you should close Mr. Fall's connection with your administration as early as possible . . . Mr. Fall's very unfortunate remarks at your inauguration have, I fear, impaired his usefulness as Attorney General.

Following the killing of Pat Garrett, Governor Curry came down from Santa Fe to attend the funeral and assist in the investigation. Participating in that investigation was another former Rough Rider named Fred Fornoff, then serving with the New Mexico Territorial Mounted Police. Although Governor Curry was convinced that Garrett had been murdered (by someone other than Wayne Brazel) as part of a conspiracy, he was unable to prove this since New Mexico at the time had "no money to extend the investigation."

After Curry's term as governor expired in 1911, he served as a Congressman from New Mexico. During World War II, Curry served on New Mexico's draft and rationing boards. Although well into his eighties, Curry also had found steady employment as New Mexico's State Historian.

George Curry died on November 24, 1948, at the age of eighty-six.

*Wayne Brazel poses
with a teddy bear
in Phoenix, Arizona,
in 1914. With him are
Elzy (left), Buster
Brown and their
wives. (Courtesy of
Jack Carter.)*

3. James Brown Miller was born on October 25, 1861, at Van Buren, Crawford County, Arkansas. His family moved to Robertson County, Texas, when he was still an infant. Jim Miller's earliest known trouble with the law began at 8 o'clock on the evening of July 30, 1884, when his brother-in-law, John Coop, was shotgunned to death while sleeping at home. Miller was accused, convicted of the crime, and given a life sentence. His lawyer won an appeal and Miller was never retried.

On March 29, 1887, Miller's friend, Emanuel "Mannen" Clements, was murdered by City Marshal Joe Townsend at Ballinger, Texas. Shortly afterward, Townsend was shotgunned by Jim Miller, but survived his wounds. The attempt at avenging Mannen Clements' death had a positive effect on the late gunman's family; on February 15, 1888, Jim Miller married Mannen's daughter, Sarah Frances "Sally" Clements, with whom he had four children.

By 1891, Jim Miller had settled in Pecos, Reeves County, Texas, where he became a deputy under Sheriff George A. "Bud" Frazer (1864-1896). Trouble between the two developed when Miller killed a Mexican prisoner in his custody. Sheriff Frazer promptly fired Miller, who soon after was appointed City Marshal of Pecos—much to Frazer's obvious displeasure. Tensions grew anew when Frazer accused Miller of the theft of a pair of mules on July 22, 1893. The case was dismissed—but Miller was fired as City Marshal.

Bud Frazer and Jim Miller shot it out—for the first time—in Pecos on April 12, 1894. Although Frazer seriously wounded Miller in the encounter, he broke and ran before the fight was finished. The second Pecos shootout between Miller and Frazer happened on December 26, 1894, with pretty much the same result—Miller was shot twice while the unwounded, and unnerved, Frazer ran for a second time. This time Frazer was charged with attempted murder, but following a change of venue, was acquitted on May 20, 1896. The feud abruptly ended on the morning of September 14, 1896, when Jim Miller killed Bud Frazer with two blasts of his shotgun in a Toyah, Texas, saloon. Miller was acquitted of the killing on the grounds that he "had done no worse than Frazer."

The acquittal hardly ended Miller's problems; when a man named Jarrett Nelson was murdered near Wellington, Texas, on August 11, 1898, Miller would be one of three men indicted for the crime. Miller was sentenced to five years, but won a reversal, and the case was dismissed. Within weeks of the dismissal, both a witness against Miller—as well as the prosecuting attorney—were murdered. Jim Miller was rumored to have had a hand in both murders, but was never actually charged with either crime.

In the dying days of the Wild West, Miller pursued his trade as a hired gun with a vengeance. He was alleged to have murdered two men in Midland County, Texas, during the summer of 1902—as well as two more men in Ward County a short time later. In addition, Miller also killed two Mexicans whom he caught butchering a steer from a herd he was guarding. A young lawyer named James Jarrott was shot four times by an assassin rumored to have been Miller—and so it went.

Miller had a very rare face-to-face encounter with T. D. "Frank" Fore in the washroom of Fort Worth's Delaware Hotel on March 10, 1904—during which Fore was mortally wounded. On May 4, 1906, Miller was acquitted of killing Fore, on grounds of self-defense. It wouldn't be long before Miller was again accused of murder; on August 1, 1906, Deputy U. S. Marshal Ben Collins was assassinated—in the style usually attributed to Miller—near Emet, Oklahoma. Although indicted and arrested, Miller was soon free on bail and would never actually stand trial for his alleged role in the murder of Ben Collins.

Miller's continued success in being released on bail, and being acquitted whenever brought to trial, was clearly due to the influence of wealthy men who employed him, and who wanted the details of their association kept private.

Ironically, the most celebrated victim attributed to Jim Miller— Pat Garrett— is one man he probably didn't kill. The reasons why, along with the remainder of Miller's story, will be given in the next chapter.

4. Cited in William A. Keleher's, *The Fabulous Frontier*, pages 72-73.

Fred Fornoff, Captain of New Mexico's Mounted Police was assigned to investigate the murder of Pat Garrett. (Courtesy of the Rose Collection, University of Oklahoma.)

EPILOGUE

The evening editions of newspapers all across Texas and New Mexico screamed the incredible news in banner headlines—although each, without fail, insisted on spelling the suspect's name as "Brazil," rather than Brazel. Typical of the massive coverage the event received was this front-page account from the February 29, 1908, edition of the *Santa Fe New Mexican:*

"PAT" GARRETT SHOT TO DEATH

Killing Takes Place Near Las Cruces.

Wayne Brazil, Young Ranchman, the Slayer.
Latter Now in Jail.

SPECIAL TO THE NEW MEXICAN—

LAS CRUCES, N. M., Feb. 29—Patrick F. Garrett, a resident of New Mexico since the latter seventies, and who sprang into fame as the slayer of "Billy the Kid" a notorious southwestern outlaw and desperado, was shot and killed about noon today by Wayne Brazil, a son of the late Captain W. W. Brazil, of Lincoln County, while on the road to the Organ mining camp in a buggy with a companion by the name of Miller,[1] at a point about five miles from here. Brazil is now in the jail at Las Cruces.

The trouble between Garrett and Brazil arose over a lease on Garrett's ranch which Brazil held. They had been quarreling along the road, Garrett being in his buggy and Brazil on horseback. Finally Brazil told Garrett that he wanted to talk to him privately.

Garrett got out of the buggy and was shot twice, one shot taking effect in his head and the other entered his chest. He expired in a few minutes.

Had a Meteororic Career

Patrick Garrett was a Texan by birth.[2] He came to Lincoln County, New Mexico, in 1878, and engaged in the cattle business. He was elected Sheriff of Lincoln County at the November 1880 election. In 1881 he started in pursuit of "Billy the Kid," one of the most notorious outlaws who ever infested the Southwest.

Billy the Kid, although only about twenty-three years of age[3] had killed over fifty men, so it was charged. That he killed more than one dozen is certain.[4]

Garrett surprised the notorious desperado at the ranch of Peter Maxwell at Fort Sumner where Billy had been hiding for several weeks.

Garrett shadowed him through a window and finding the door ajar, stepped in with his pistol ready. Billy the Kid endeavored to get his Winchester but was too slow and was shot and killed by Garrett.

Known as Fearless Officer

After several years of residence in the county of Lincoln, Garrett removed to Dona Ana County where he was appointed sheriff to serve an unexpired term of the sheriff who died and was elected for the next term.[5]

Thereafter he was captain of a company of Texas Rangers in counties adjacent to New Mexico. He served also for a term of four years as Collector of United States Customs in El Paso, Texas, which office he left after the expiration of his term of service about two years ago. Since then he has been engaged in mining in Chihuahua, Mexico, and in the Organ Mountains.

Was a Dead Shot

He leaves a widow and two children.[6] Garrett was noted as one of the most skillful and successful hunters of criminals for many years in New Mexico and Texas and was a dead shot with both the revolver and rifle and whenever he drew a bead on a man it was either give or be killed.

In appearance he was a typical Texan, stood six feet two[7] with not a superfluous ounce of flesh on his body, clean shaven except for a mustache, fair complexion, brown hair and with a face that expressed determination and pluck and he was one of the most noted characters of the Southwest for a number of years.

George Gaither (center) and Sheriff James H. Boone (right) of El Paso in about 1900. (Courtesy of Martin Merrill.)

Honored By President Roosevelt

He was appointed Collector of Customs by President Roosevelt to whom he was introduced in Washington by Judge Albert B. Fall. The President took a great fancy to him and gave him the important position because President Roosevelt is a great admirer of good shooting.

Immediately after the news of Garrett's death, Governor George Curry rushed to Las Cruces from the capital. Curry was accompanied by James M. Hervey, New Mexico's Attorney General, and Captain Fred Fornoff[8] of the New Mexico Territorial Mounted Police.

Governor Curry talked to many persons in Las Cruces, publicly and privately, to find some deeper motive than Wayne Brazel's claim that he had shot in self-defense. Despite days of effort, neither Curry nor Hervey was able to unearth any evidence that would prove that anyone but Brazel was involved in the murder.

Further investigation by Captain Fred Fornoff, however, disclosed a spent Winchester rifle cartridge near the Garrett murder site. This, coupled with a report that the notorious Jim Miller was seen in the area shortly after the killing, has led the overwhelming majority of historians to conclude that Garrett was actually shot from ambush by Miller. While the majority may be comfortable with this notion . . . the evidence suggests otherwise.[9]

Pat Garrett's funeral was held on the afternoon of Monday, March 2, 1908, and was attended by hundreds of his friends and neighbors. Prior to his burial, he had lain in state at Strong's Undertaking Parlors, an establishment that was forced to send to El Paso for an extra large casket to accommodate Pat Garrett's 6'5" frame. Until the long coffin arrived, Garrett's body was stretched out across five chairs.

The deceased's two brothers, John and Alfred Garrett of Haynesville, Louisiana, were the only blood relatives to attend the funeral—other than his children. In his will, Garrett had left instructions that absolutely no religious rites should be connected with his passing, and that wish was honored. A long procession followed the hearse to the Odd Fellows' Cemetery on the outskirts of Las Cruces. The pallbearers included his old friends, Governor George Curry and former Deputy Collector of Customs, Numa Buchoz.

Another pallbearer—Tom Powers—shocked those at the graveside when he read the famous eulogy that Robert G. Ingersoll had written on the occasion of his brother's death some thirty years earlier. Both Garrett and Powers were atheists and admirers of Ingersoll. While the graveside gathering may not have agreed with the philosophy, they were visibly moved by the eulogy which concluded with the lines:

> And now, to you, who have been chosen from among the many men he loved, to do the last sad office for the dead, we give his sacred dust. Speech cannot contain our love. There was, there is, no gentler, stronger, manlier man.

Shortly after Garrett was laid to rest, the Santa Fe *New Mexican* of March 2, 1908, hit the streets with this front page story of Pat's murder and an account of his funeral:

GARRETT SLAIN IN SELF DEFENSE

Attempted to Shoot Brazil But Was Too Slow

Dispute Caused Tragedy

Coroner's Jury Holds Killing Was Justified

Funeral Held Today.

SPECIAL TO THE NEW MEXICAN.

LAS CRUCES, N. M., March 2.—Patrick F. Garrett, who was shot and almost instantly killed near this city on Saturday last, fulfilled his own prophecy that he would "die with his boots on." Late developments show that the killing of Garrett was a plain case of self-defense and while his death is generally deplored, there is little feeling of bitterness against Wayne Brazil, the young ranchman who did the shooting.

At the time he met his death, Garrett was returning to his home in Las Cruces from a visit to one of his Organ Mountain ranches. He was riding in a mountain buckboard with a man named Edmonson (sic). They were overtaken about four miles from here by Brazil who was riding on horseback.

Words passed between the two men regarding the violation of a contract held by Brazil on Garrett's ranch, and finally, according to Edmonson, the sole eyewitness to the tragedy, Garrett, who had already climbed out of the buckboard and was standing on the ground, reached for his shotgun in the bottom of the vehicle, saying: "God Damn you, if I can't get you off my ranch one way, I will get you off another."

As he pointed the gun towards Brazil, the latter instantly drew a 45-Colts six-shooter and fired twice in quick succession. One bullet entered Garrett's left breast, passing through his heart and the other struck him in the center of the forehead piercing his brain. Death was practically instantaneous.

Slayer Surrendered to Sheriff.

Brazil then turned his six-shooter on Edmonson and demanded that he take him at once to Las Cruces and tell the story of the shooting exactly as it happened under penalty of death. The body of Garrett was left lying by the roadside, where it was found several hours later, with the shotgun which caused his death, clasped in his arms.

Immediately on reaching town, Brazil surrendered to Sheriff Lucero and was locked up in the county jail. Aside from the cool declaration that the killing was done in self defense he refused to discuss the tragedy.

At the coroner's inquest Edmonson corraborated Brazil's story in every detail and the jury returned a verdict that Garrett came to his death as a result of gunshot wounds inflicted by Brazil in self-defense.

The news of Garrett's death created intense excitement in Las Cruces, but since the facts have become known this has subsided. A widow and two children are left to mourn his death.

Funeral of Garrett Held Today

The funeral of Garrett was held here today and was largely attended. Among those in attendance at the services were a number of old friends of the deceased from El Paso, Texas. Burial was in the village cemetery. Mrs. Garrett is prostrated as a result of the tragedy and is under the care of a physician.

Brazil is still in jail. He has employed Judge Albert B. Fall, formerly Attorney General of the territory, to defend him. He will apply for bond should he be held to the grand jury on the charge of murder.

Jesse Wayne Brazel was released on March 4, 1908, on $10,000 bail. His trial was still more than a year in the future. On the same day that Brazel was released on bail, Emerson Hough wrote this letter of condolence to Apolinaria Garrett:

This was Pat Garrett's home in Roswell, New Mexico, in 1898. (Courtesy of James Shinkle.)

March 4, 1908.

Senora P. F. Garrett,
Organ P. O., New Mexico.

My dear Senora Garrett:

In this time of your sorrow, I don't know whether you care to hear from any one at all, but I thought you might like to have a few words of sincere sympathy at this time.

I knew your husband well. He was a brave and noble man. I am as sure as though I had seen the whole deed, that he was never killed in any fair encounter. I know how averse he was to going armed or starting any kind of quarrels.

Now that my friend is gone, I cannot tell you how sad and lonely it leaves me feeling. I wish he might have lived out his life with you all and have succeeded in every ambition he ever entertained.

This news is inexpressibly shocking to me. I send you my greeting and regard to you and all your children. I had hoped to see you all at your home some time. Please tell Poe[10] to write to me and give me the particulars of his father's end. I only saw the newspaper reports, which are not always accurate.

Believe me

Truly your friend,

EMERSON HOUGH

Along with Governor George Curry, Emerson Hough also believed that Pat Garrett had been the victim of an assassination plot. Hough expressed these feelings to President Theodore Roosevelt and received this brief, and to-the-point, reply:

March 6, 1908

My dear Mr. Hough:

I feel just as you do, that Pat Garrett was murdered. I was very sorry to hear that he was dead.

Sincerely yours,

THEODORE ROOSEVELT

It was several months before Pat Garrett's distraught wife could bring herself to acknowledge Emerson Hough's letter of condolence. Pat's murder had left his family in worse financial shape than ever. We can only imagine the thoughts that must have been running through the desperate Mrs. Garrett's mind as she penned this plea for aid:

Organ, N. Mex.
June 10, 1908

Mr. Emerson Hough
Chicago, Ill.

Dear Sir and Friend:

No doubt I must be the slowest among your many correspondents and I admit that I certainly owe you a humble apology for delaying so long in answering your kind and beautifully sympathetic favor of a late date. However I think I am entitled to some consideration (due to) the terrible loss to myself and family.

The most kind and loving husband and father loved by all law abiding and honest citizens, disliked and feared by the lawless and murderous elements on account of his loyalty to justice. Consequently the atrocious plot that resulted in his untimely death.

I cannot go into detail of this awful crime, but I will have Poe write you more definitely in the near future. Certainly there is a just God who must meet out justice to such cold blooded murderers.

We are getting on fairly well. Tis very dry out here. We have a nice little garden and our stock are doing well. I wish to sell out. You know what a ranch we have and about two hundred head of good horses and cattle.

Relative to the *Story of the Outlaw* of which you are author, I desire to ask as an interested party whether or not you can render me any assistance financially from that source. I am very much in need of money and if the book has done any good I would highly appreciate a remittance.

My taxes are over due and I must make some arrangements to pay same. Tis extremely hard to obtain money here on acct. of money panic. Can't even sell cows or horses for anything like their value.[11]

Kindly write me at your earliest convenience. Lizzie has an appointment from the board of trustees of the Blind Institute in Alamogordo as Superintendent and to take effect in September. Isn't that fine?[12]

Annie is employed in El Paso as a saleslady in Popular store. Poe is here with me on the ranch. The family joins me in love to Mrs. Hough and yourself.

Sincerely yours,

MRS. P. F. GARRETT

As usual, Emerson Hough was long on encouragement and short on cash—as his last letter to the Garrett family illustrates:

June 18, 1908.

Mrs. P. F. Garrett
Organ, New Mexico.

Dear Mrs. Garrett:

I am glad to hear from you, and I wish I could help you, but the truth is that Pat has had as much out of this book as I have. At first I thought of making it altogether on the Southwest and Billy the Kid, but, as you know, my publishers would not stand for that alone, and I re-wrote the book, covering the whole country.

In this Pat did not help me, and there was never any partnership in regard to the book, but what I gave him was a part of the advance money paid by my publishers and in return for assistance he rendered me.

I am glad the girls are well situated, and only wish that the rest of you need have no uneasiness about money matters. I cannot tell you how much I was grieved to hear of the untimely end of your husband and my friend.

Sincerely yours,

EMERSON HOUGH

A letter written to Emerson
Hough in June of 1908
by Mrs. Pat Garrett.
(Courtesy of the Iowa
State Historical Department.)

Organ N. mex
June 10, 08

Mr. Emerson Hough
Chicago Ill

Dear Sir and Friend
No doubt I must be the slowest among your many correspondents and I admit that I certainly owe you an humble apology for delaying so long in answering you kind and beautifully sympathetic favor of a late date. However I think I am entitled to some consideration the terrible loss to myself and family The most kind and loving husband and father loved by all law abiding and honest citizens. disliked by

and feared by the lawless and murderous element on account of his loyalty to justice Consequently the atrocious plots that resulted in his untimely death I cannot go into detail of this awful crime but I will have Poe write you more definitely in the near future Certainly the is a just God who must mete out justice to such cold blooded murder We are getting on fairly well 'tis very dry either we have a nice little garden and our stock are doing well I wish to sell out you know I about what a ranch we have and about two hundred head of good horses and

cattle. Relative to the story of the outlaw of which you are Author I desire to ask as an interested party whether or not you render me any assistance financially from that source I am very much in need of money and if the book has done any good I would highly appreciate a remittance my debts are over due and I must make some arrangements to pay same tis extremely hard to obtain money here on acct of money panic can't even sell cows or horses for anything like their value

Kindly write me at your earliest convenience Lizzie has an appointment from the board of Trustees of the blind Institute at Alamogordo as superintendant to take effect in September 1st that find Anne is employed in El Paso as saleslady in Popular store Poe is here with me on the ranch The family joins me in love to mrs Hough and yourself
Sincerely yours
mrs P. F. Garrett

Jim Miller, who many believed killed Pat Garrett, is shown hanging at the left after his lynching in Ada, Oklahoma, in 1909. (Courtesy of the Rose Collection, University of Oklahoma Library.)

On February 27, 1909—just two days shy of the first anniversary of Pat Garrett's death—Jim Miller was back in the news. On that day, Allen Augustus "Gus" Bobbitt was shot and killed from ambush near Ada, Oklahoma. Jim Miller, John Williamson (Miller's nephew) and Oscar Peeler were charged with the murder of Bobbitt on March 1, 1909. Testimony implicated two more men—Jesse West and Joe Allen—who allegedly paid Miller $2,000 for the killing, as well as providing him with another $3,000 in the event of his capture. In addition, a certain Berry B. Burrell was implicated as being the intermediary between Miller and Allen and West.

Arrests quickly followed. Burrell was arrested in Fort Worth on March 12; Miller was next on March 30 and finally West and Allen on April 8, 1909. A preliminary hearing was held in Ada on April 15. Peeler and Williamson turned state's evidence, and were transferred to a jail at Tecumseh, Oklahoma. Miller, Burrel, Allen and West were confined to jail at Ada without bail.

Jarvis P. Garrett, Pat's youngest son is shown holding one of his father's guns in 1972. (Courtesy of Robert McNellis.)

At two o'clock in the morning of April 19, 1909, a mob of Ada citizens cut the town's telephone communications and stormed the jail. The four prisoners were quickly taken to a livery barn at 117 North Townsend Street. The mob strung up Jesse West first, followed by Joe Allen and Berry B. Burrell; Jim Miller was saved for last. When the mob tried to get Miller to confess his various crimes, he snapped: "Just let the record show that I've killed fifty-one men."

Miller then calmly removed his diamond ring, asking that it be sent to his wife in Fort Worth. After a few parting remarks, Miller himself commanded: "Let 'er rip!" . . . and the mob quickly obliged.

The other major suspect in the murder of Pat Garrett was finally brought to trial on May 4, 1909. Jesse Wayne Brazel was represented at his trial by Albert B. Fall, who seemed to have developed a talent for playing a leading role in the key events of Pat Garrett's final years. On the witness stand Brazel asserted that he had shot only when his own life was in jeopardy—that is, when Garrett supposedly pulled a shotgun on him.

Significantly, the sole eye-witness—Carl Adamson—never appeared at the trial; a fact which conspiracy buffs have construed as conclusive evidence that Garrett had indeed been the victim of an assassination plot. The trial lasted just one day. After a fifteen-minute deliberation by the jury, Brazel was acquitted.

Following his trial, Brazel bought a ranch and got married. His wife died of pneumonia in 1911, and Brazel finally sold his ranch on February 27, 1913. Jesse Wayne Brazel was last seen during May, 1914—although speculation abounds, no one really knows what became of him after that date.

The debate over how Pat Garrett was killed is as heated today as it was in 1908. Everyone has a pet suspect and good arguments to support his cause; it is doubtful, however, that the mystery will ever be resolved to everyone's satisfaction. All that is certain is that Garrett was given no more chance to defend himself than he gave Billy the Kid. But to Garrett's credit, Billy the Kid was not shot from behind.

1. Garrett's actual companion was Carl Adamson—but the reference to Jim Miller is interesting, to say the very least.

2. See Chapter Three, Note 1.

3. The many theories concerning Billy the Kid's antecedents were discussed in great detail in my November, 1978, *Real West* article, "The Search for Billy the Kid's Roots." The riddle finally was resolved, to the satisfaction of most historians—and obviously this one—with the publication of my follow-up article, "The Search for Billy the Kid's Roots—Is Over!" which appeared in the January, 1980, issue of *Real West*.

That article proved conclusively, and in great detail, that the future Billy the Kid was born as Henry McCarty at 210 Greene Street, in New York City on September 17, 1859. Thus, at the time of his death Billy the Kid was exactly 21 years, 9 months and 27 days old. Interested readers seeking further information are advised to consult both *Real West* articles.

4. The victims that can be ascribed to Billy the Kid are as follows:

Frank P. Cahill—mortally wounded by the Kid on August 17, 1877.

Frank Baker, William S. Morton and William McCloskey—killed by a group of eleven "Regulators," including the Kid, on on March 9, 1878.

Sheriff William Brady and George W. Hindman—shot and killed by a group of five concealed assailants, including Billy the Kid on April 1, 1878.

Robert W. Beckwith—killed by the Kid on July 19, 1878.

Joe Grant—shot and killed by the Kid on January 10, 1880.

James Carlyle—killed during a fight between Billy the Kid and two companions and a posse on November 29, 1880. Historians have never resolved whether posseman Carlyle was killed by the Kid and his friends or by accident at the hands of his fellow lawmen.

Robert Ameridth Olinger and James W. Bell—shot and killed by the Kid on April 28, 1881.

5. Garrett was not "appointed sheriff to serve an unexpired term of the sheriff who died." The fact is that Pat Garrett was elected Sheriff of Lincoln County, New Mexico, on November 2, 1880, having defeated his opponent—incumbent Sheriff George Kimball by a vote of 320 to 179.

6. Garrett actually had eight children.

7. Garrett was at least 6'4" and possibly 6'5" in height.

8. Fornoff had served with Governor Curry in the Rough Riders.

9. Jim Miller's usual weapon was a shotgun, not a Winchester. Certainly this particular Winchester cartridge was never traced to Miller, nor was he ever charged with the crime. A good case can be made for any of several suspects depending on which "authority" one chooses to believe. Interestingly, the Garrett family always maintained that the actual assassin was Carl Adamson.

Garrett's most recent biographer, Leon C. Metz, presented a very logical argument as to why the killer of Pat Garrett was probably the man no one wants to believe it was—Jesse Wayne Brazel.

10. "Poe" refers to Pat's 22 year-old son, Dudley Poe Garrett.

11. Economists have divided the "business cycle" into four phases: prosperity, liquidation, depression and recovery. At the time Mrs. Garrett wrote her letter, the lowest points of major U. S. business cycles had been hit in 1858, 1861, 1867, 1879, 1885, 1894 and 1908. As far as the financial well-being of his family was concerned, Pat Garrett couldn't have died at a worse time.

12. Elizabeth "Lizzie" Garrett was born in 1885. Blind from birth, she became a noted composer and singer and close friend of Helen Keller. She died in 1947 at age 62 when she was struck by a car in Roswell, New Mexico.

THE
EARLY WEST

SOURCES

As long ago as 1952, the published works on the subject of Billy the Kid had become numerous enough to inspire a bibliography of some 437 items. Since then, the list has more than doubled. It is highly unlikely that any lengthy bibliography will ever be required for the man who killed Billy the Kid. Less than a handful of books, devoted to Pat Garrett's entire career, have been published—with only one of them worth talking about.

The one worth talking about is Leon C. Metz's *Pat Garrett: The Story of a Western Lawman* (University of Oklahoma Press, 1974).

We still know very little about Garrett's role as a husband and father. We know very little, also, about the few close friendships he had—including the most famous one of all with Tom Powers. With luck, a future historian may uncover a cache of documents that will provide a key to the real Pat Garrett. Until then, here is the list of sources for letters and documents that have been reproduced in *Garrett and Roosevelt*.

Microfilm print-outs of the following letters, quoted in *Garrett and Roosevelt*, are available from the Microtext Division, Widener Library, Harvard College, Cambridge, MA 02138:

Reel and Series

December 16, 1905	Theodore Roosevelt to Emerson Hough	340-2
December 19, 1905	Emerson Hough to Theodore Roosevelt	61-1
December 22, 1905	Theodore Roosevelt to Emerson Hough	340-2
March 6, 1908	Theodore Roosevelt to Emerson Hough	348-2

Copies of the following letters, quoted in *Garrett and Roosevelt*, are available from the Iowa State Historical Department, East 12th and Grand Avenue, Des Moines, IA 50319:

June 30, 1904	Emerson Hough to Pat Garrett
January 3, 1905	Emerson Hough to Pat Garrett
March 29, 1905	Emerson Hough to Pat Garrett
May 2, 1905	Emerson Hough to Pat Garrett

July 19, 1905	Emerson Hough to Pat Garrett
July 25, 1905	Pat Garrett to Emerson Hough
December 26, 1905	Emerson Hough to Pat Garrett
January 6, 1906	Emerson Hough to Pat Garrett
February 7, 1906	Emerson Hough to Pat Garrett
February 7, 1907	Pat Garrett to Emerson Hough
February 12, 1907	Emerson Hough to Pat Garrett
July 2, 1907	Pat Garrett to Emerson Hough
March 4, 1908	Emerson Hough to Apolinaria Garrett
June 10, 1908	Apolinaria Garrett to Emerson Hough
June 18, 1908	Emerson Hough to Apolinaria Garrett

Copies of the following letters and telegrams, quoted in *Garrett and Roosevelt* are available from the National Archives and Records Service, Washington, D. C. 20408 and can be found in Record Group No. 56:

December 5, 1901	Frank Cox to Theodore Roosevelt
December 12, 1901	George A. Knight to Theodore Roosevelt
December 12, 1901	C. W. Murray to Theodore Roosevelt
December 12, 1901	M. B. Hawkins and J. H. Mason to Theodore Roosevelt
December 12, 1901	Charles A. Boynton to Theodore Roosevelt
December 12, 1901	S. B. Strang to Theodore Roosevelt
December 12, 1901	William E. Dwyer to Theodore Roosevelt
December 12, 1901	Theo. Miller to Theodore Roosevelt
December 12, 1901	D. B. Hoarnbeck to Theodore Roosevelt
December 12, 1901	A. M. Morrison to Theodore Roosevelt
December 12, 1901	Cecil A. Lyon to Theodore Roosevelt
December 12, 1901	T. J. Darlin to Theodore Roosevelt
December 13, 1901	George A. Knight to Theodore Roosevelt
December 13, 1901	C. C. Flanagan to Theodore Roosevelt
December 13, 1901	Joe E. Williams to Theodore Roosevelt
December 13, 1901	J. A. Smith, et al to Theodore Roosevelt
December 13, 1901	George Ogden to Pat Garrett
December 13, 1901	L. N. Hiel to Pat Garrett
December 13, 1901	L. N. Hiel and friends to Pat Garrett
December 13, 1901	L. W. Evans to Pat Garrett
December 13, 1901	R. F. Campbell to Pat Garrett
December 13, 1901	C. M. Foraker to Pat Garrett
December 13, 1901	R. F. Campbell to Pat Garrett
December 14, 1901	B. S. Rodey to George B. Cortelyou
December 14, 1901	Pat Garrett to B. S. Rodey
December 14, 1901	International Exchange Bank to Theodore Roosevelt

December 14, 1901	J. M. Hawkins to Theodore Roosevelt
December 14, 1901	B. F. Hammett to Theodore Roosevelt
December 14, 1901	H. L. Newman to Theodore Roosevelt
December 14, 1901	S. J. Frendenthall to Theodore Roosevelt
December 14, 1901	J. A. Eddy to Theodore Roosevelt
December 14, 1901	James G. Lowdon to Theodore Roosevelt
December 14, 1901	Cecil A. Lyons to Theodore Roosevelt
March 12, 1901	H. E. Delaney to Theodore Roosevelt
April 7, 1903	Pat Garrett to Leslie M. Shaw
May 14, 1903	R. Achon to Pat Garrett
May 18, 1903	William H. H. Llewellyn to Leslie M. Shaw
May 22, 1903	J. H. Biggs to I. A. Barnes
May 22, 1903	J. C. Peyton to I. A. Barnes
May 22, 1903	George M. Gaither to I. A. Barnes
May 22, 1903	Pat Garrett to I. A. Barnes
May 27, 1903	I. A. Barnes to Leslie M. Shaw
May 27, 1903	Joseph F. Evans to I. A. Barnes
May 27, 1903	Maury Kemp to I. A. Barnes
November 5, 1904	J. A. Smith to Leslie M. Shaw

The following newspapers quoted in *Garrett and Roosevelt* are available on microfilm through inter-library loan:

El Paso *Herald*	December 12, 1901
El Paso *Herald*	December 13, 1901
El Paso *Herald*	December 14, 1901
El Paso *Herald*	December 16, 1901
El Paso *Herald*	December 19, 1901
El Paso *Herald*	December 26, 1901
El Paso *Herald*	December 27, 1901
El Paso *Times*	August 27, 1902
Houston *Post*	March 11, 1903
El Paso *Herald*	May 8, 1903
El Paso *Evening News*	May 8, 1903
El Paso *Herald*	December 9, 1905
El Paso *Herald*	December 12, 1905
El Paso *Herald*	December 13, 1905
El Paso *Herald*	December 20, 1905
El Paso *Herald*	December 21, 1905
El Paso *Herald*	December 25, 1905
El Paso *Herald*	December 26, 1905
El Paso *Herald*	January 2, 1906
Santa Fe *New Mexican*	February 29, 1908
Santa Fe *New Mexican*	March 2, 1908

A quartet of historians gather at Tombstone, Arizona's O.K. Corral on June 15, 1980. Left to right are Alford E. Turner (author of THE EARPS TALK and THE O.K. CORRAL IN-QUEST), Robert F. Palmquist (author of numerous articles), Jack DeMattos, and Glen G. Boyer (author of AN ILLUSTRATED LIFE OF DOC HOLLIDAY, SUPPRESSED MURDER OF WYATT EARP, I MARRIED WYATT EARP, and many other publications. This photo was taken by Bill Kelly, author of the ENCYCLOPEDIA OF GUNMEN.

ABOUT THE AUTHOR

Jack DeMattos' interest in Theodore Roosevelt's "White House Gunfighters" began with a casual visit in 1975 to Harvard College—the repository for more than 100,000 letters to and from Theodore Roosevelt. Jack was hoping to find "one or two" letters between Roosevelt and one of the noted gunfighters he befriended. It turned out that hundreds of these letters existed between the well-known (and not so well-known) gunfighters and Theodore Roosevelt.

Limiting the list to the three most interesting "White House Gunfighters" was no easy task since there was a rather large group to choose from. That selection has now been made. The first volume of the "White House Gunfighters" trilogy, *Masterson and Roosevelt* appeared in 1984, this second volume is devoted to Pat Garrett, while a third and final volume will concern the least known—but perhaps most interesting of all— Ben Daniels.

An artist by vocation and a writer by avocation, Jack DeMattos was born in Providence, Rhode Island, on July 26, 1944. He makes his home in North Attleboro, Massachusetts, with his wife, Sandi, and their two children, Dawn and Greg. After graduating from the Art Institute of Boston in 1966, Jack became a free-lance artist who attracted national attention for his caricatures, drawn from life, of such show-business personalities as Joan Collins, Sammy Davis, Jimmy Durante, Jayne Mansfield, Mary Tyler Moore and Barbra Streisand.

Jack is the author of more than seventy articles which have appeared in such publications as *True West, Frontier Times, The Tombstone Epitaph,* and *Real West.* Since 1979, he has served as Historical Consultant for *Real West* and has written and illustrated the critically-acclaimed "Gunfighters of the Real West" series for that magazine. *Garrett and Roosevelt* is his third book.

INDEX

THE
EARLY WEST

THEODOR

President of the Un

To all to whom these

Know Ye, *That, reposing special trust and con*

Patrick

I have Nominated, and by and with the ad

Collector of Customs for the District of

and do authorize and empower him to execute and fulfil th
the said Office with all the rights and emoluments thereun
during the term of Four years from the *date her*
and duly qualified.

In Testimony Whereof

Treasury Department of the t

Given under my ha

in the year of our

Independenc

twenty-six th.

By the PRESIDENT.

Secretary of the Treasury.